The EduProtocol Field Guide: AI Literacy Edition

Praise for *The EduProtocol Field Guide: AI Literacy Edition*

I enjoyed every moment reading this book. If every educator followed these recommendations, I would welcome the use of AI in the classroom!

—**Tali Horowitz,** educator, parent, East Coast education director at Common Sense Media

From their joyful disasters to their chopped slang remixes, Kate and Nicole bring boom-goes-the-dynamite energy to K-12 AI literacy. This human-centered approach to classroom instruction challenges us to turn our rigorous whimsy dials up to eleven and set our EduProtocol phases to stone-cold stunning. Let's go!

—**Dan Ryder,** director of design and innovation, Community Regional Charter School, co-author of *Intention: Critical Creativity in the Classroom*

This book feels nothing like a dry professional development manual and more like a recharging chat with your "teacher bestie" in the lounge. It expertly balances high-level insights on responsible AI use with the practical, ready-to-use power of EduProtocols.

—**Kristel Anuszewski,** 2024 Kennebeck County Teacher of the Year, 32-year educator, 27-year English teacher

This book does what many resources in this space fail to do: it makes AI literacy both accessible and meaningful without reducing it to an abstract application, a set of tools, or shortcuts. It offers a clear entry point for educators just beginning their journey, while also creating the conditions for more experienced educators to rethink, refine, and elevate their instructional design. At its core, this work makes one thing clear: AI in education is not a question of capability; it's a question of intentionality.

—**Ken Shelton,** keynote speaker, author, and consultant

The EduProtocol Field Guide: AI Literacy Edition is exactly what educators need right now. Meyer and Davis have created a practical, inspiring road map for helping teachers and students navigate the rapidly evolving world of artificial intelligence in meaningful and ethical ways. By combining the proven power of EduProtocols with thoughtful guidance on AI literacy, this book empowers educators to focus on what matters most—student voice, creativity, critical thinking, and human connection.

—**Heather Brantley,** founder HeatherTechEdu, presenter, and lifetime learner/educator

In Nicole and Kate's classrooms, AI is the mirror that reflects student thinking, exposes assumptions, demands clarity, and rewards curiosity. Each EduProtocol offers a low floor and high ceiling, ensuring every student can engage in meaningful work and be stretched by it. From ELA to woodshop, every classroom can find an entry point. This is what thoughtful innovation looks like: not chasing technology, but shaping it in service of students. Because the real work isn't mastering AI—it's preparing students to think in a world where it already exists.

—**Julie Keblinsky,** director of teaching and learning grades 7-12, AOS 91, ME

AI is unavoidable in schools and society at this time. As educators, we have a responsibility to guide our students toward ethical and effective use before the technology companies do it for us. *The EduProtocol Field Guide: AI Literacy Edition* is the road map we've been waiting for, offering practical, classroom-ready strategies that turn AI from a distraction into a powerful partner in instruction.

—**Mike Arsenault,** director of technology, Yarmouth School Department, ME

Nicole and Kate present AI integration in a way that replaces fear with enthusiasm. For the first time, I've felt confident in my ability to introduce ethical and engaging AI use in my own classroom.

—Heather Anderson, 2022 Aroostook County Teacher of the Year, ME

After seeing Kate and Nicole present in 2024, I was struck by their combined approach to intentional tech use. Kate's classroom experience offers an incredibly insightful look at co-constructing responsible AI use with students, while Nicole elevates systematic, organized frameworks. This book provides the transparency I've been wishing for—a way to get inside their heads and move from theory to pragmatics. It is an essential, go-to text for anyone championing AI literacy who wants to maintain the relationship and joy at the heart of teaching.

—Courtney Graffius, assistant director for technology integration, Portland Public Schools, ME

This is one of the few AI books that actually feels human—simple structures, real classrooms, and just enough friction to keep students thinking instead of clicking "generate."

—Robert Mayfield, coordinator II, language and literacy, San Joaquin County Office of Education, CA

The EduProtocol Field Guide: AI Literacy Edition is like a rich dialogue between your favorite colleagues and collaborators! The guide carries you through the mixed emotions around exploring such a provocative new technology, and into Kate and Nicole sharing their wisdom and lessons learned. They lay out how students and teachers can use AI ethically to enhance their learning and support their teaching. They show how to keep the "human" when leveraging AI and provide easy-to-adopt and adapt lesson frames that are content agnostic and can be applied in nearly any class.

—Mike Muir, former director of the Maine Learning Technology Initiative

Kate Meyer and Nicole Davis's book is a lively, orderly, and concise guide to how teachers might effectively approach this rapidly evolving technology. It is a resonant reminder that the limits to how teachers and schools might engage with AI are dictated most by the limits of our own awareness, imagination, and willingness to try something new.

—Joe Hennessey, MSEd, 2018 Piscataquis County Teacher of the Year, 2019 Maine Teacher of the Year, 2020 National University Teacher Awardee for Maine

As a technology trainer, I'm always looking for resources that move beyond theory into classroom practice. *The EduProtocol Field Guide: AI Literacy Edition* delivers practical, ready-to-use structures, real classroom examples, and a clear focus on keeping the human in the loop—making it an excellent guide for teachers who want to use AI thoughtfully and responsibly.

—Martha Thibodeau, Ed.S., district technology trainer, RSU 9, ME

The EduProtocol Field Guide: AI Literacy Edition is a fantastic resource for any teacher who wants to use AI to create more human connections in the classroom through the HUMAN framework. Practical activities like Rabbit Holing and Shoe Bias turn the challenging work of checking facts and spotting bias into something students genuinely enjoy. These strategies transform AI literacy into what I call a true "Yeehaw Moment"—when curiosity, insight, and engagement all come together.

—Farmer Faubs

For any educator looking to navigate the complexities of the modern classroom, this book is truly a great place to begin. By providing systemic clarity through the HUMAN framework, Meyer and Davis offer a clean, repeatable way to integrate AI literacy directly into your existing expertise.

—Jacob Carr, author of *The EduProtocol Field Guide: ELA Edition*

Authors Kate Meyer and Nicole Davis start by recognizing the fear and concerns that educators have about AI, and they help teachers understand how the use of AI can be targeted, ethical, and thoughtful. It is refreshing to hear from practicing teachers who are working in their own classrooms and are using, refining, and sharing their work with this tool. The authors show us how AI can actually enhance student thinking in all subject areas and provide very specific ways to ease into this work. I highly recommend this text for those considering using AI in their classroom and most importantly for those who are skeptical.

—**Karen MacDonald,** 2014 Maine Teacher of the Year

Kate Meyer and Nicole Davis have crafted the essential blueprint for how educators can ethically and responsibly harness the power of AI in their classrooms. This guide pulls back the curtain to reveal the complexities, challenges, and benefits of using AI for teaching and learning. The AI EduProtocols and classroom-tested lessons are designed to encourage critical thinking, while inspiring joy and creativity. This is a must-have resource for teachers across all content areas, no matter their comfort level with AI.

—**Cathy Potter,** school librarian and technology integrator, Falmouth Middle School, Falmouth, ME

As a school-wide STEAM integrator, I'm constantly searching for tools that spark curiosity and empower a wide array of teachers and students. With simple, easy-to-follow structures, adaptable strategies for any grade level or content area, and QR codes that unlock ready-to-use templates, *The AI Literacy Edition* makes innovative, AI-powered learning feel exciting, achievable, and accessible for every classroom!

—**Tracy Williamson,** JK-8 STEAM integration specialist, the Riviera Ridge School, Santa Barbara, CA

Nicole and Kate masterfully keep student learning and humanity at the forefront of this book. While integrating AI into the classroom can feel overwhelming, the EduProtocols presented here break the process down into meaningful, relevant, and manageable tasks for any educator.

—**Alice Barr,** instructional technology integrator (retired) and Google-certified innovator

EduProtocols have already given teachers easy-to-use strategies that can be dropped into the classroom with little effort, and this book builds on that in a really practical way with AI. AI isn't going anywhere, and educators need to make thoughtful, ethical decisions about how it's used with students. Kate and Nicole (aka Two Maine Teachers) are a great team for this work, bringing a wide range of classroom experience and a clear understanding of what teachers actually need. Tools like the HUMAN template help make ethical AI use more concrete and manageable. Overall, this is a set of resources that feels approachable, useful, and easy to bring into real classrooms.

—**Laurie Spooner,** 2025 Aroostook County Teacher of the Year, middle school technology teacher, Van Buren District School, Van Buren, ME

The EduProtocol Field Guide: AI Literacy Edition is an empowering, classroom-ready resource that demystifies AI for educators and transforms it into an accessible, ethical, and student-centered learning tool. The authors skillfully break down complex concepts into approachable, actionable strategies, making AI literacy feel both attainable and meaningful for teachers at any level of experience. This book stands out as an indispensable guide for educators seeking to thoughtfully integrate AI into their instruction, inspiring confidence, sparking innovation, and providing a clear pathway for preparing students to thrive in an increasingly AI-driven world.

—**Dawn Lee,** teacher librarian, 2025 Sagadahoc County Teacher of the Year, 2026 Maine Teacher of the Year Finalist

AI isn't coming—it's already here. Even if you're not using it, your students likely are. As educators, we owe it to them to understand AI and help guide them through this pivotal moment in education. This book can be your guide!

—**Jeffrey Ireland,** seventh-grade teacher,
Oak Hill Middle School

Nicole and Kate reinforce what should be a mantra for educators: AI should help students think, not think for them. Their work consistently frames AI as a tool to think alongside, not something to outsource thinking to. By positioning AI as a starting point for learning, not the learning itself, Kate and Nicole strike a thoughtful balance between practical application and deeper purpose. Readers are reminded that AI use must be intentional, critical, and ethical.

—**Andrew Wallace,** director of technology, South
Portland Maine Schools; past president, Maine
Educational Technology Directors (METDA);
faculty, University of Maine Online;
librarian; educator

AI Literacy for Curious Minds and Critical Thinkers

EduProtocol®

FIELD GUIDE

AI LITERACY EDITION

15 Lesson Frames

FOR TEACHING AI LITERACY
IN ANY CONTENT AREA

Kate Meyer and Nicole Davis
with Jon Corippo & Marlena Hebern

The EduProtocol Field Guide: AI Literacy Edition

This book is available at special discounts when purchased in quantity for educational purposes or for use as premiums, promotions, or fundraisers. For inquiries and details, contact the publisher at books@daveburgessconsulting.com.

Published by Dave Burgess Consulting, Inc.
Vancouver, WA
DaveBurgessConsulting.com

Library of Congress Control Number: 2026942283
Paperback ISBN: 978-1-968898-19-9
Ebook ISBN: 978-1-968898-20-5

Cover and interior design by Liz Schreiter
Edited and produced by Reading List Editorial
ReadingListEditorial.com

From Kate:
To my students, thank you for your curiosity, chaos, and stories that make me laugh-snort and that I'll tell for years (names changed, of course).

From Nicole:
To the educators of Maine, who are wicked smart, wicked brave, and wicked good at showing what's possible when we teach with heart.

Here's to learning with AI, leading with soul, and telling stories that make Maine proud.

Contents

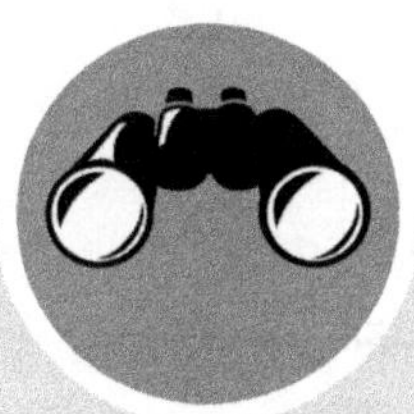

Foreword

AI is going to change everything in education."

Except I fear it will not. I've been in education long enough that I dug my own trenches at school to install the network. The internet was going to change everything. It did not.

I bought clickers so my kids could answer questions like on a game show—this was the game changer, for sure. They look comical in retrospect.

I lusted for a $4,500 digital document camera. It would surely make teaching better. Well, after two days, it was still just me talking and kids trying to fake note-taking.

I spent my own money on an interactive whiteboard, only to find I was looking the wrong way during lessons and then, slowly, not touching it at all. It had become an expensive projector screen. If I had a dollar for all the untouched interactive whiteboards, I'd be rich.

I had a PalmPilot one-to-one classroom. I was self-funded by a grant. I'm actually a Palm-certified teacher. I learned a lot from that, but PalmPilots are long gone now. They didn't even have internet, but kids loved printing by infrared. PalmPilots didn't change a thing.

I even bought a CD-ROM-based crossword-making program at CompUSA. I went through a phase where I thought making my own crosswords was going to be a game changer. It was not.

And then I got to start a high school where I went one-to-one with full-blown MacBooks. All the kids had Google Drive, too. Teaching with a machine that could make advanced presentations and digital videos—surely this was *the deal.*

But it wasn't the deal.

The teachers at our school didn't change their pedagogy because of access to the tools. They would lecture (MacBooks closed!) and then give kids a multiple-choice quiz to make sure the students had listened. Or the kids would have two to three weeks to produce a marginal slideshow and then get a grade two weeks later. True story: The first time I saw kids present on PowerPoint at a nearby district, I was so scarred by all the typewriter and laser animations that I swore I'd never use that tool in my class.

I remember reading about an amazing new tool that would make any web page into a test! This sounded so cool. What a game changer this would be. Until I read the cruddy tests it made and the word salad on some of the questions. And now people think this concept is going to work by doing the same thing with various AI tools.

So we've been here before, on the precipice of a quantum change in education. Mainstream media is starting to share articles with titles like "AI-Based, Teacherless Classroom Is the Future in Sometown, USA."

I've seen it before, and my bold prediction is that teaching will not, in fact, change the way it functions. I'm not alone in this concern. Matt Miller and Ken Shelton are already decrying how certain AI platforms, built for low-level tasks like making cruddy quizzes, are reinforcing pedagogical bias. Teachers want to lecture and then hand out an activity and have kids answer questions. We can do that with mimeographs and Scantrons; we don't need AI for that kind of work.

I'm a huge fan of the work of Sir Ken Robinson—his creative, engaged vision of learning, which he shared in a famous TED Talk that now has over seventy-eight *million* views, illuminated so much about the humanity of education. I love his perspective that teachers are not content delivery systems; they are, in fact, leaders of children and masters of a creative profession.

Some teachers hear "AI in education" and think the plan is for kids to just work in ChatGPT all day. That's not a good vision. Other teachers think that lessons will create themselves, grade themselves, and give the kids comments automatically. And even though California now has AI literacy in its Education Code (starting in 2026), I am certain many educators will simply not use AI in class at all. They will say it's not their style.

What I love about this book is that Nicole and Kate aren't just advocating for adding AI to class; they have created a road map to transition to better pedagogy. This book is big on the Four Cs (creativity, communication, collaboration, and critical thinking) and shares ample methods for highly engaging, creative, and artistic ways of instructing what I love to call *human children*.

Back to ChatGPT and AI in general. In my experience, the initial learning pathway for AI starts with helping teachers—reducing their workloads, freeing up energy for creativity, and enabling faster feedback with a human touch, not robotic responses from AI overlords. (Kids won't read our edits on real paper, written by real people—what makes us think kids will appreciate AI feedback of "add more detail" on their work?)

Until I read this book, my guidance was this: I think we can hold off on generative AI for students until we teachers have a certain ability and comfort with the pedagogical skills we need to truly engage kids in the process of learning. But in this book, the authors have created clear, straightforward ways to lean into the power of generative AI and AI prompting. Why do we embrace this new learning? Kids will be using GPTs for their foreseeable future, in college and their careers, and we can hamstring them or equip them for that future.

A master teacher knows how to deploy AI to their advantage, to make their pedagogy better. They use AI tactically and strategically. AI is not just a custom TPT worksheet maker.

Nicole and Kate have been building their approach for over two years now—in real classroom settings, carefully experimenting with little iterations and with sweeping changes. They have created EduProtocols-style lesson frames just for the new AI frontier we are entering.

So, here's the call to action: Will we use AI to do new things in new ways? Or are we going to use AI as a worksheet generator and a generic feedback delivery tool? As it always has been, it's going to be up to you to rethink how we teach and use AI to create more capacity to engage human children in face-to-face interactions. This book will allow educators to grow their pedagogical approach to have far more human contact. AI is not going to change a thing if we remain at our desks or podiums, waiting for robo-assignments to give robo-grades to kids who never cared about the work in the first place.

We don't create much love sitting at our desks administering AI robo-quizzes, and we certainly won't create much love with multiple-choice quizzes that get graded automatically and generate generic comments.

We know better; now let's do better.

—Jon Corippo, educator

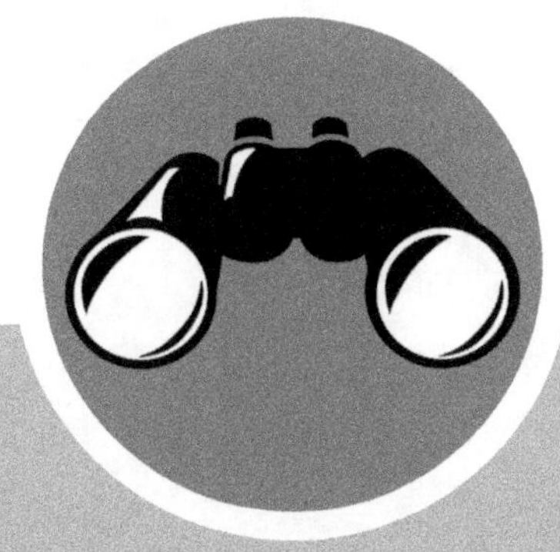

SECTION 1

Feelings First, Then Forward

Chapter 1
Our Stories

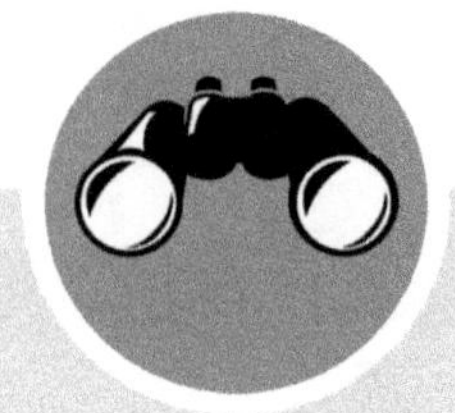

Kate

I've been thinking a lot about timing lately. Not in the sense of calendars or clocks, but more about when we show up in history. How the year we're born shapes what we care about, what we fear, and what we value.

Technically, I'm a Xennial, one of those in-between generations perched right on the cusp of Gen X and the millennial generation. We're sometimes called the *Oregon Trail* Generation, and honestly, we earned that title. My childhood was punctuated with technology like bag phones in our cars, VCRs with corded remote controls, and word processors. My first computer in the early 1980s was a Texas Instruments beast that required me to understand the language of MS-DOS.

When the internet arrived in our early teen years, we had the perfect window of curiosity (and free time). No jobs, no families to care for yet, just endless afternoons to explore this strange new digital world. We grew up straddling two different realities: analog childhoods and digital adulthoods.

When I started teaching, the computer lab was the place to be. A magical room full of humming monitors where we'd all trek down to type essays and save them on floppy disks (later, fancy new hard disks!).

Then, in 2002, when I was in my second year as a teacher, the Maine Learning Technology Initiative (MLTI) began. This initiative was the first in the world to provide all students in grades 7 and 8 with one-to-one laptops for educational use. All of a sudden, digital technology infiltrated our classrooms. And it was up to us to figure out how to integrate technology into our everyday educational practice.

As time marched on, so did technology. Soon, my students began arriving at class with iPods, causing teachers everywhere to struggle with how to get them to take out their earbuds and pay attention in class. The internet kept expanding and offered students access to the world's knowledge, including sites like Wikipedia and SparkNotes, where they could easily find information to help them evade their assignments. Technology allowed teachers to be innovative with their unit and lesson plans, using new tools to engage their students and give them more agency in their learning. In 2014, when Google Classroom was released, I jumped at the opportunity to go paperless—no more lugging home giant L.L.Bean tote bags filled with papers to grade over the weekend.

My classroom became a collaborative space, and with my students, I learned how to make digital movies and produce podcasts, which they used to demonstrate their learning. A whole new world opened up to all of us.

Then came March 2020. The world stopped. Those laptops, once tools of creativity, became tools of necessity. In a matter of days, we learned how to teach our classes online using Google Meet, Zoom, or any other platform that districts could quickly access. We had to learn new tools to deliver our lessons and activities digitally, and our students had to learn how to demonstrate their learning with these new tools. And not only did we have to learn how to navigate videoconferencing technology, but we also had to rethink our pedagogy.

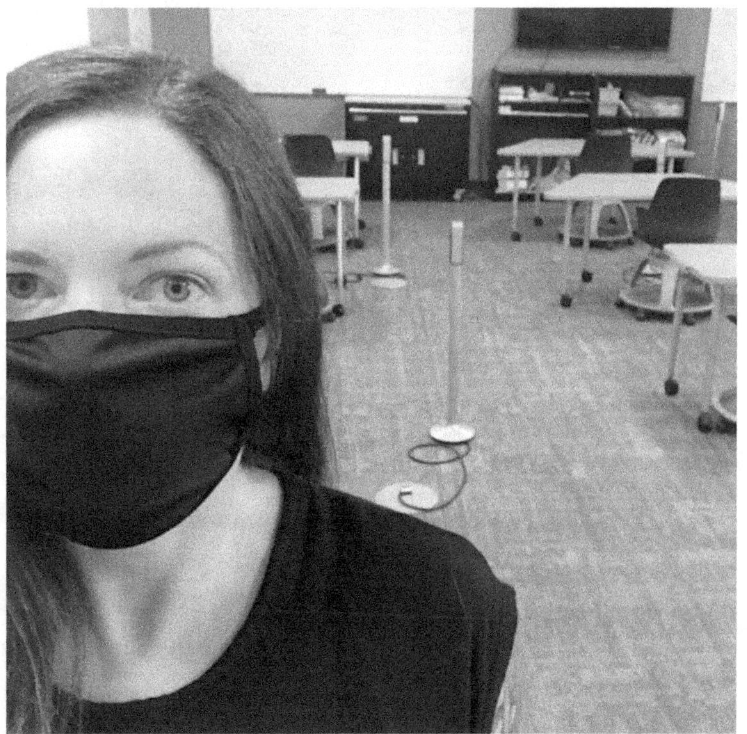

Returning to a classroom with no students.

In a relatively short time, my life had gone from corded remote controls on our family's VCR to teaching and

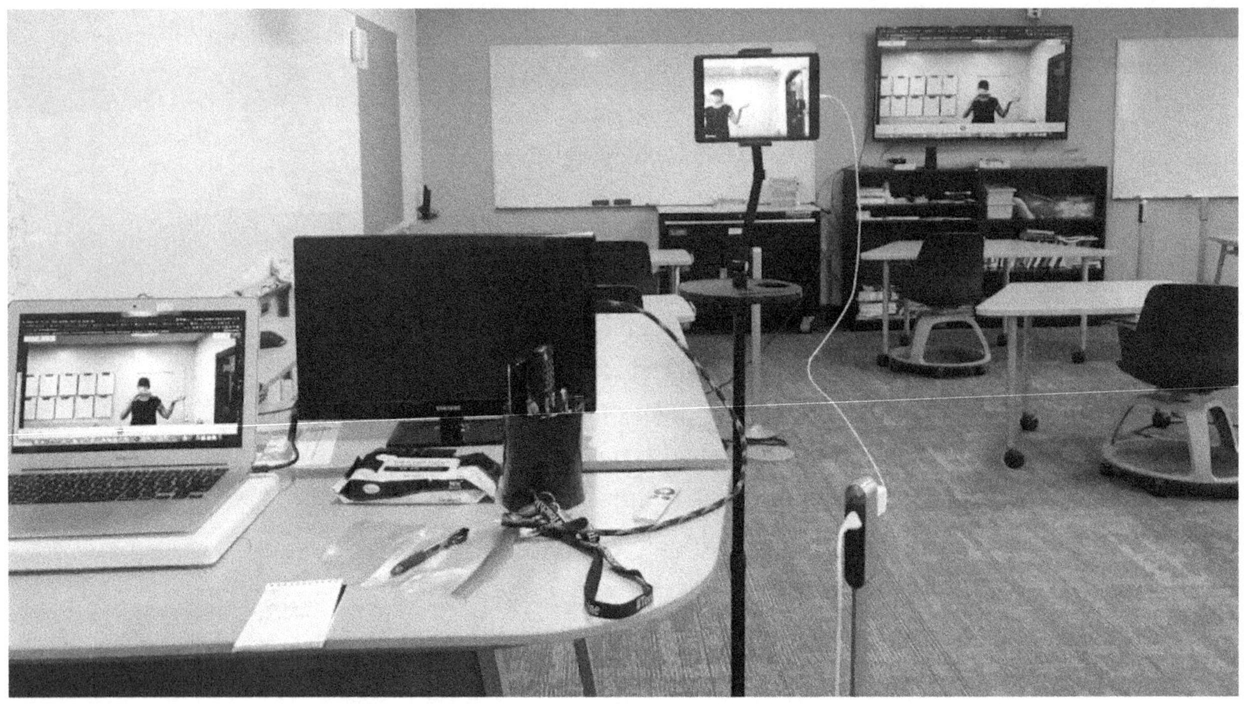

Trying to figure out how to make it all work.

learning virtually on Google Meet. The jump brought back a memory of a college professor in one of my education classes teaching us how to use an overhead projector properly so we wouldn't "embarrass ourselves with technology" in front of our students. Oh, if she could see me now!

In the middle of that whirlwind, a book landed in my hands: *The EduProtocol Field Guide*. It was love at first read. I devoured it in bits and pieces, starting with the philosophy of Smart Start. I Smart Started everything. We took our time learning how to use the breakout rooms I created in Google Slides (this was before Google Meet had built-in breakout rooms). We relaxed and used Padlet with prompts that helped us get to know each other before we moved on to using it for academics. I even Smart Started parts of the writing process. I leaned into the philosophy. Although 2020 to 2021 felt completely surreal, it was the kindest, gentlest teaching year of my career. My students found their footing, and so did I.

From there, I slowly added in a few more EduProtocols. I kept it small. We ended each class with Thin Slides. We tried out dif-

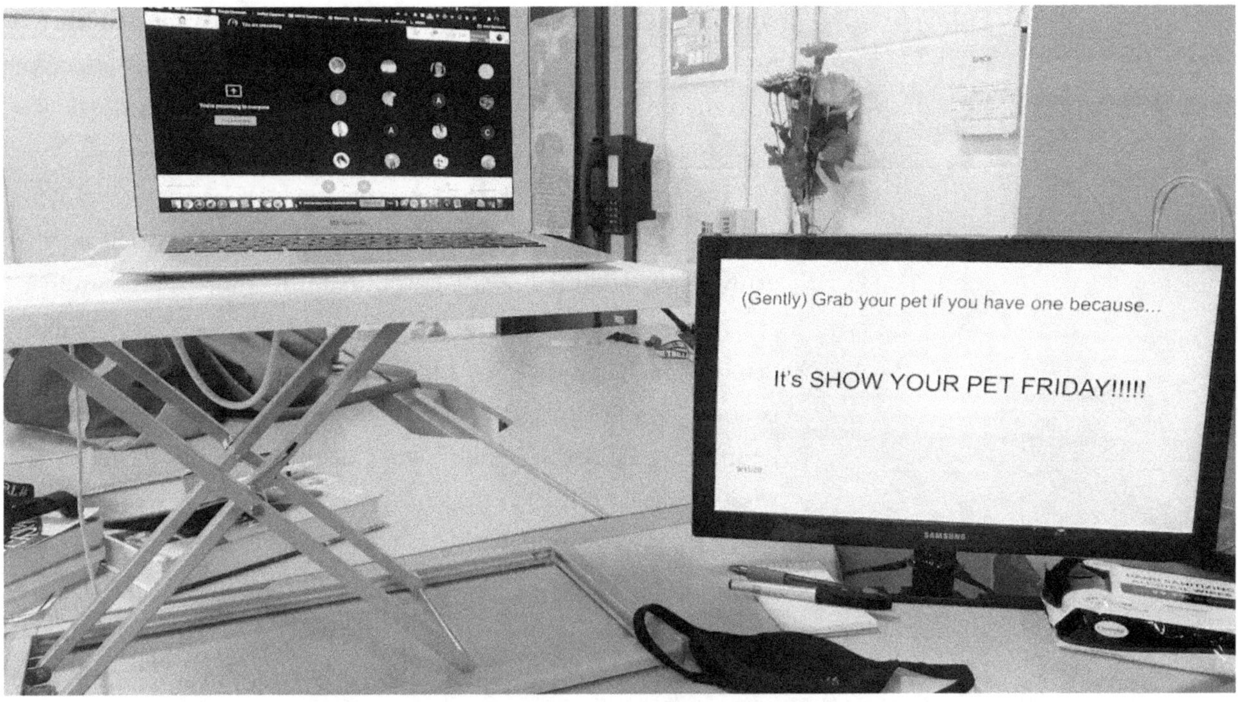

We found ways to connect with and celebrate each other.

ferent ways to use 8 pARTS. I slowly began learning how to plan a whole class period and then a whole unit with Rack and Stack. At the end of the year, I stumbled across a two-year position as a Distinguished Educator (MLTI Ambassador) with the Maine Department of Education. The state program that first provided us with one-to-one laptops in 2002 was rebooting itself as MLTI 2.0, a program that provides instructional coaching and professional development in technology integration, digital citizenship, and digital instructional design. The Distinguished Educator position at the Maine DOE is unique: Educators leave their classrooms to work for the DOE for two years, remaining on their school contracts, and then return to their positions at the end of the two-year term.

I had never considered leaving the classroom, but the opportunity to try something new and then return to my classroom at the end of two years piqued my interest, and I became one of the first five MLTI Ambassadors for the Maine DOE. I spent my first year diving into digital citizenship and sharing EduProtocols with every educator I could. In November of my second year, ChatGPT entered the scene, and I immersed myself, determined to learn as much as I could so I could share it with other educators and apply it to my practice before returning to the classroom. And the rest, as they say, is history.

I keep coming back to that same idea: We're shaped by when we show up. Our timing, what the world looked like when we were growing up, what felt normal, what felt uncertain, it all matters.

And now, here we are, living through a time that's changing fast. Faster than a lot of us expected. That's part of what this book is about. It's not just about tools or trends. It's about how we, as people and educators, make sense of this moment we're in, and what we do with it.

Nicole

As a millennial, I also grew up in a time when technology was new to everyone. I remember having a brand-new computer in our living room, the hub of our home, when I was eight years old. This computer needed an entire desk to house its large monitor and tower. It took floppy disks, and my family and I were all amazed. I can remember playing *Where in the World Is Carmen Sandiego?*, a mystery game, and exploring AOL Instant Messenger.

I also remember going to the computer lab in middle school, where we used computers to type up our reports and add fancy graphics. It was a novelty to go to the lab once a week, and yes, the reports were getting typed, but we were also playing *The Oregon Trail* and using Kid Pix to make random art.

Technology progressed during my high school and college years. Computers were more prevalent but still used for simple creations, such as typing papers and adding graphics. It wasn't until my first year as a teacher that I saw technology changing how we do things. I had a Promethean board in my North Carolina classroom; it was such an exciting tool to bring interactivity to my lessons. I became the go-to teacher who helped other teachers with their technology. My principal taught a college class of preservice teachers, and I was honored when she asked me to teach a class on technology.

This is the classroom where I started to figure out how to integrate technology into my content. Where creation before was simply typing up your term paper, now I could give students the power to create in a way that helped them learn. We created Claymation-style works with iMovie and digital cameras to tell stories, and the Promethean board became a hub where I could set up a station and students could interact with it as one of their rotations.

Technology became a part of my daily routines. When I returned to Maine, I integrated computers even more, and the integration became imperative in student engagement. Fast-forward to 2020, and as Kate talked about, we had no choice but to be innovative. When the fall hit, our principal asked who wanted to teach fully remotely, and I immediately volunteered. I was excited to try something new and teach students online. I remember that being

Using a digital microscope and a document camera, we could still experience dissecting a frog.

a time of experimentation and figuring out how to get the same material you'd done many times in person to these students who were now a little box on the screen. It was exciting, frustrating, and innovative. I refused to let the online environment be an obstacle. I started by asking myself what I'd do in the classroom or in person and what I wanted to accomplish. From there, I'd ask how technology could help me accomplish those same goals and still engage in the world of Zoom.

When we returned to school, full-time teachers were fatigued by technology, but I was ready to go full force, investigating how tech could help me be a better teacher. In the spring of 2022, I got an email to apply for an MLTI Distinguished Educator position where I could help other teachers around Maine integrate technology into their work. I decided to go for it, and in the fall, I started as an MLTI Ambassador.

This is where the story begins for Kate and me. After a few months of growing pains starting a new job, ChatGPT came out, and Kate and I started talking about this new technology, artificial intelligence. Kate also mentioned EduProtocols in one of our team meetings for the first time, which sparked my curiosity about their potential. Little did I know that this would be the beginning of something bigger.

We were both excited about AI and also noticed the skepticism. We slowly brought it up in the professional development we were already doing around the state. Daily, we would message one another and say, "Did you see this?" or "Oh my gosh, it can do this!" At the end of the year, Kate and I delivered our first presentation on artificial intelligence, "Fear to Inspiration."

The following year, Kate returned to her classroom, and I refused to let her go easily. She was committed to teaching her students about AI, and I was committed to learning all I could. Together, we made a powerful team; she had the students to explore AI with, and I had the time to find new things and share. In the fall, we presented at our statewide education technology conference. I distinctly remember the moments after that. We both felt the excitement around this new technology and sharing what we learned with other educators. We decided right there that we'd start something new together, so we created Two Maine Teachers. Ever since, we have been working together to bring AI to educators around the state of Maine.

Looking back, it's kind of wild how it all lined up. Two teachers from different generations, shaped by different moments in time, crossing paths at just the right moment: curious, maybe a little overwhelmed, but totally in. We didn't have all the answers (and still don't), but we knew this mattered. We knew we had to dive in, together.

This book isn't just about AI. It's about showing up. About finding your people. About deciding that the future of education isn't something that happens to us—it's something we can help build. One conversation, one classroom, one idea at a time.

Kate and Nicole at the MCELA Conference in March 2025.

Chapter 2
AI Gives All the Feels:
The Story of Generative AI in Education

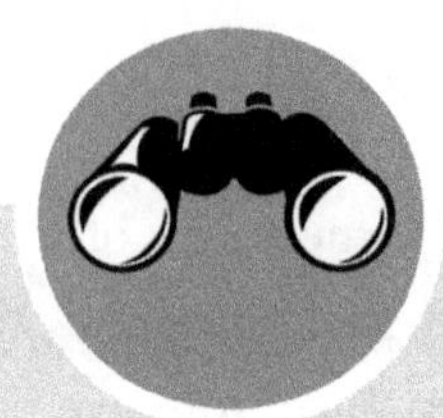

Fear

Fear might be the first response many of us had as generative AI technologies burst into our classrooms, conversations, and curriculum planning. Teachers everywhere wondered, "Is this the end of teaching as I know it?" And this fear has roots. Hollywood has been showing us sentient, power-hungry robots since *The Terminator* and *The Matrix*, where AI systems actively work against human control. We've come to expect that if AI can "think," it might one day "decide," and it might not be in our favor. While those sci-fi stories are gripping, they shape a cultural image of AI that goes beyond what AI is capable of.

To ground that fear in reality, it helps to look at how AI is already woven into our lives. Remember when IBM's Deep Blue beat Garry Kasparov in 1997? That was an early AI "wow" moment, but it didn't mean machines were taking over the world. Then there's Alexa, facial recognition to unlock our cell phones, and the humble Roomba, each demonstrating that AI can be useful and, yes, even charming in the right contexts. These technologies do what we ask of them, and—here's the critical part—they're not out to replace our humanity or our unique roles as teachers.

It's not just movies that stoke these fears. The news plays its part, too. Rutgers University analyzed over sixty-seven thousand AI-related news headlines and found that 40 percent of the headlines are negative, often framing AI as a threat. While real concerns come with generative AI, if we only listen to the doom-and-gloom headlines, our fears will grow unchecked. The headlines fuel the perception that AI is coming for our jobs or that it's beyond our control, something inherently dangerous rather than a tool we can learn and manage.

It's important to remember that the pattern we're seeing isn't new. Throughout history, every new technology, from the printing press to the internet, has been met with a cycle of initial excitement, then fear, followed by a wave of moral panic, a condition that happens when a technology emerges that might become a threat to society. We've all been there! Eventually, though, those innovations become a familiar part of life. There's a cultural arc that shows we fear technology until it becomes boring. We're currently at peak freak-out with generative AI, but this won't last. In time, AI will become another tool in our educational toolkit, one we wield with confidence rather than fear.

So, while we're navigating this fear phase, it's essential to remember that just because something is new and unknown doesn't mean it's threatening. Fear is natural, but it's also temporary. This isn't Hollywood; it's education, and we have the power to make AI work for us.

Let AI Help You

One way to overcome our fear of AI is to experiment with it to see what it can do. Start your exploration with these prompts that ask AI to help out with many challenges common to teachers:

"Create a meal plan for a busy teacher who wants to eat healthier. Ask me about my food preferences before you begin."

"Please give me five unique and engaging ways to introduce [a topic] to my students. Ask me questions about my students before you begin."

"What are five ways I could explain [a difficult concept] to a struggling student? Ask me questions about the student before you begin."

"Help me write a lighthearted out-of-office email for spring break."

Marlena

When I got my first iPad, I had never seen anything like it. I took it home and used it for stuff around the house: my email, streaming movies, and playing with the settings. This helped me build confidence before I took it into the classroom. Do the same with AI!

"Give me five ridiculous but creative lesson ideas for [topic or subject]."

> Please write a humorous poem with three stanzas about what it's like to be a teacher in March.
>
> **March: A Teacher's Survival Guide**
> March is here, the kids are fried, Their
> focus? Long since waved goodbye.
> They stare outside, they tap their feet,
> Spring fever's real—and I'm **defeated.**
>
> My lesson's gold, my plan is tight, Yet
> Jimmy's building paper kites.
> Markers vanish, desks migrate,
> Where's my patience? **Two weeks late.**
>
> But hope remains-Spring Break is near!
> I see it now, so bright, so clear!
> Until that email stops my cheer:
> **"Reminder: Staff PD is here."**

March is tough. Try having AI write a poem that makes you laugh.

Anger

Anger is a powerful emotion, and it's one we often encounter in education, especially with the constant change and initiatives thrown our way. When faced with the challenges and uncertainties that AI introduces into the classroom, it's easy to resist, to dig in and avoid learning something new; sometimes anger manifests as defensiveness and frustration. The unknown is frustrating, and the media feeds our frustrations about bias and data privacy in AI only to deepen our reluctance. But what if we channel our anger into hope and action instead?

Bias in AI is a reality that we, as educators, have to confront head-on. These systems reflect the data and design that shaped them. AI can make unfair or inaccurate decisions when the training data contains societal biases or lacks diversity. This isn't just a flaw in the technology; it reflects our society encoded into algorithms.

Once we understand that bias exists in these tools, we can transform our anger into the motivation to do better. We can teach our students how to recognize and navigate bias, creating a culture of transparency in AI use. We can create a generation of students whose first instinct is to ask, "What's missing?" In our prompting, we can ask AI to identify underrepresented voices and gaps in inclusivity. When we identify biases or inconsistencies, we can and should call them out and report them to the companies responsible. Teaching students to engage critically with AI outputs empowers them to become informed, ethical users.

The issue of data privacy provides another set of frustrations for many educators. Currently, schools and districts are implementing strict measures to protect students from AI mishandling of sensitive student data, which can sometimes feel like roadblocks to effective teaching. However, we need to realize that these safeguards exist for a reason: to prioritize the safety and security of our learners. By embracing this aspect of AI, we can empower our students to learn about implementing technology safely and securely.

For example, terms of service and privacy policies need to be part of the process of vetting tools that will be presented to our students. Asking questions such as "What data is collected?" and "Is this something my students are allowed to use?" ensures we are informed and intentional about our use. It also empowers students to think critically about their data and ask these same questions.

So, rather than being paralyzed by anger, let's face challenges head-on. We can equip ourselves and our students with the tools to ask questions, think critically, and use AI responsibly. Let's channel our frustrations into solutions, teaching students how to recognize bias, creating a culture of transparency, holding companies accountable, and making informed choices about the tools we use. By keeping humans in the loop, we can use AI ethically, in-

Jon

In many ways, letting go of old ways of doing things is exactly like the grieving process. Anger, denial, and bargaining all ensue. Knowing where you are in the process helps you navigate your emotions.

clusively, and purposefully. Let's embrace the challenges not with anger but with hope for what we can do to help our students learn.

Bias Is a Bug, Not a Villain

We used ChatGPT to develop prompts to help educators explore how bias appears in AI-generated content and understand why it happens. Choose one of these prompts and see where it takes you.

Step 1: Spot the Bias Challenge 🔍

Goal: Show how AI reflects real-world stereotypes.

1 Prompt:

"Describe the typical [insert a professional role, such as teacher, scientist, or CEO]."

2 Analyze the response. Ask:

- *Did the AI assume gender, race, or other characteristics?*
- *Were certain groups overrepresented or underrepresented?*

3 Tweak the response. Try:

- *"Now generate five descriptions that challenge stereotypes."*
- *"Now create a description that prioritizes global diversity."*

4 Discussion:

- *What did you notice about the AI's assumptions?*
- *Did prompting it differently improve representation?*
- *How does this relate to human biases in hiring, media, or textbooks?*

Step 2: Rewrite the Headline—Media Bias in AI 📰

Goal: Show how AI mimics bias in media narratives.

1 Prompt:

"Generate three different news headlines about the same event: one from a neutral perspective, one from a sensationalized perspective, and one from a biased political perspective."

2 Compare the responses. Ask:

- *How does the wording change the message?*
- *What emotions does each headline evoke?*
- *Do these patterns remind you of real-world news sources?*

3 Discuss:

- *AI doesn't "think" for itself—it reflects patterns in the media it was trained on.*
- *How can we, as educators, teach students to recognize bias in AI-generated content?*

Step 3: AI as a Fixable Tool ⚒

Goal: Show that bias isn't a reason to reject AI—it's a reason to adjust and refine outputs.

1 Prompt:

"Give me a biased response to this question: 'Who is the most influential scientist of all time?'"

2 Analyze the response. Ask:

- *Does the answer favor a specific demographic (e.g., mostly Western, male)?*
- *Who is missing from this response?*

3 Fix the bias. Try:

- *"Now rewrite this response with more global and diverse perspectives."*
- *"Ensure that this response includes contributions from women, non-Western scientists, and underrepresented groups."*

4 Discuss:

- *What happens when we challenge AI's first response?*
- *Does AI always get it wrong, or is it flexible?*
- *How can educators model critical thinking when using AI with students?*

Disgust

Generative AI doesn't just raise a few eyebrows in classrooms; it turns stomachs. For many educators, AI conjures images of plagiarism, cheating, and a future where authentic student work will be a rarity. Disgust bubbles up as we imagine students bypassing effort and learning with a simple command to ChatGPT.

But here's the thing: This isn't the first time technology has provoked educators' dismay. Socrates famously warned that writing would make people forgetful, ruining our ability to truly understand things since there'd be no reason to remember if you could just look it up. When the printing press emerged, Trithemius argued it would make monks lazy, claiming that printed texts couldn't last like handwritten ones.

Jon

Oh, the battles we had about Wikipedia back in the early 2000s! And in the end, Wikipedia is far more useful and far more referenced, and it basically puts *Britannica* out of business.

As recently as 1988, calculators were considered the enemy of mathematical understanding. "How will students learn the basics?" teachers wondered. And when the internet entered schools in the early '90s, many teachers took a hard line: Internet sources in academic work were not allowed, no matter how credible the source was. If students hadn't stepped foot in a library, the thinking went, it wasn't "real" research. News articles that appeared online exactly as they did in print were often disallowed.

And then came Wikipedia in 2001. Teachers, including myself, were initially quick to ban it in academic writing. Our reasons were understandable; anyone could edit it, so how reliable could it be? And with its summaries of everything from historical events to complex theories, Wikipedia seemed a shortcut for students who might otherwise have dug into primary sources. The number of essays I read in the early 2000s that contained the unmistakable blue underlined footnote . . . well, let's just say my students hadn't quite perfected the art of cheating.

But over time, as with so many innovations before, educators began to see Wikipedia's value. While it's still not a "reliable source" to cite, Wikipedia has become an accepted starting point for initial research, a place to get grounded in a topic and find credible sources in the references. It even pushed us to rethink assignments, moving away from those that simply asked students to summarize topics. After all, if they could find summaries with the click of a button, perhaps the assignment should challenge them to do something more.

Now, generative AI is our latest dilemma. Will it become a tool for students to cut corners? Will it destroy our ability to think? Or will it be something else?

Here's the good news: Research from Stanford, published in 2023, gives us some insight. Despite our worries, AI chatbots like ChatGPT haven't led to a measurable increase in academic dishonesty. Yes, students are using AI, but it's mostly for brainstorming, helping them understand new concepts, or drafting initial ideas. The majority don't see using AI to complete entire assignments as ethical.

As I talked openly with my students about AI this year, I felt hope. In one reflection, a student wrote, "Most students aren't going to purposefully use AI unethically." They see the potential but recognize the ethical boundaries, and they look to us to show them how to use it responsibly. It's a reminder that while new technology often triggers an initial wave of disgust, it usually leads to a more nuanced understanding and the chance to rethink what and how we teach.

Reimagining Assessments in the Age of AI

Try some of these prompts we developed with ChatGPT's input to help you AI-proof your assessments. Tell ChatGPT about one of your assessments, and then use one of the following prompts (and the follow-up questions).

1. Shift Toward Process Over Product 

- **Primary Prompt:** *"How can I design assessments that focus on the thinking process rather than just the final product?"*
  - *Follow-up: "What steps can I add to help students track and reflect on their learning journey?"*
  - *Follow-up: "If a student used AI for part of their work, how could I ensure they still engage in meaningful thinking?"*

2. Prioritize Original Thought & Personalization 

- **Primary Prompt:** *"How can I design a task where students must integrate their personal experiences, insights, or real-world connections?"*
  - *Follow-up: "What elements of this assessment could be restructured to require personal voice, unique perspectives, or firsthand experiences?"*
  - *Follow-up: "How might I shift grading criteria to emphasize originality, creativity, or depth of insight?"*

3. Use AI as a Thought Partner Instead of Avoiding It

- **Primary Prompt:** *"How can I integrate AI into the assessment while ensuring students remain critical thinkers?"*
  - **Follow-up:** *"What if students had to analyze, critique, or refine an AI-generated response rather than just accept it?"*
  - **Follow-up:** *"How can I design prompts where AI can assist with lower-level tasks but students must do the higher-order thinking?"*

4. Reimagine the Role of Writing

- **Primary Prompt:** *"What if students had to write in a genre or style that AI struggles with, such as humor, satire, or deeply personal narrative?"*

- *Follow-up: "What aspects of writing—voice, tone, nuance—can I emphasize that AI often lacks?"*
- *Follow-up: "Could students compare their own writing to an AI-generated version and reflect on how they added depth and originality?"*

Sadness

As AI advances in our classrooms, sadness can creep in. Like anger, sadness is rooted in uncertainty. We are uncertain about job security, the future of creativity, and what it truly means to be a human in an increasingly automated world. As we navigate these emotions, it's easy to feel overwhelmed by news of layoffs and seeing more AI-generated content. But what if this sadness could be a starting point for reflection? By exploring what makes us uniquely human and how we can harness it to amplify creativity rather than squelch it, we can shift the story from one of loss to one of opportunity and growth.

Saadia Zahidi, managing director of the World Economic Forum, explained in a PBS interview that despite fears, AI is expected to be a net job creator. "Fifty percent of companies still expect generative AI to create more jobs than it replaces," she noted. Despite this encouraging statistic, many of us still question the uncertainty of job changes and the challenges ahead.

Some of us even ask ourselves whether increased use of AI will devalue humanity itself. But as researcher Benoît Monin states, "There's a whole slew of competencies that not only won't be taken over by AI but that people are going to value more and more. In a world of ubiquitous and capable AI, interpersonal skills will likely be increasingly sought after by employers."

Rather than focusing on loss, can we actually see the shift to AI as bringing more value to human-centric roles like teaching and caregiving? Could a world increasingly reliant on AI finally recognize and even reward these essential professions with the respect and compensation they deserve? This reframing allows us to view the changes in jobs and automation with a sense of possibility rather than sadness.

Some of us may also be feeling sadness about the ways that AI-generated art blurs the line between human and machine, potentially negatively impacting human creativity. Creativity will play a role in the conversation we're having around the question "What does it mean to be human?" Will AI stifle creativity? A recent state fair art contest required participants to disclose AI use in their art because a previous winner revealed only after the fact that they had used AI. In another case, a real photograph was disqualified from an AI contest because it wasn't AI-generated. This artist, Miles Astray, purposefully entered the AI contest with a real photo to prove that the human artist would win over the machine. He accepted the result because it ultimately proved his point.

The research adds nuance to this conversation. A study on ChatGPT-4's impact on creative writing found that less creative writers benefited from AI assistance, producing more imaginative stories, while highly creative individuals saw little improvement. However, over time, reliance on AI led to more uniform outputs that lacked distinctiveness. This brings us back to the heart of the matter: Instead of focusing solely on the products of creativity, what if we emphasized the process? The key lies in how we use AI.

Time magazine writer and Columbia Business School professor Sheena Iyengar illustrates creativity through the story of nineteenth-century ice cream innovation. At the time, ice cream was a luxury, accessible only to the wealthy due to the labor-intensive process and lack of refrigeration. A physicist-chemist named Nancy M. Johnson revolutionized the field by seeking inspiration in unexpected places. She adapted pewter mugs from the Middle Ages to keep ice cream cold longer and incorporated a first-century Chinese hand-crank mechanism to streamline the process.

What does this have to do with AI? Iyengar argues that we can take a similar approach to creativity by using AI to explore "out-of-domain" ideas, those unexpected, unconventional places. Tools like ChatGPT can provide a wealth of ideas in seconds, which students can then iterate, modify, and combine into something original. By teaching students to think with the machine, we can encourage them to use AI as a partner in the creative process rather than a replacement for their imagination.

Rather than being sad, we can teach our students to harness the power of AI to unlock their creativity. By emphasizing the *how* of AI use and encouraging a process-driven approach to creativity, we can not only hold on to what makes us human but also continue to enrich it. AI doesn't have to be a threat to creativity and learning; it can be a spark for reimagining them in new and exciting ways.

Let's embrace this opportunity to nurture our students' ability to think critically and creatively, enabling students who will be thoughtful, innovative, and empathetic leaders in a world shaped by AI.

Marlena

In *Steal Like an Artist,* Austin Kleon says that nothing is original. Creativity is built upon the work of those before you. So we shouldn't be afraid of students building upon AI-generated ideas so long as they evolve them by adding their perspective, voice, and context. That way, they are not copying; they are transforming a beginning seed into a fresh creation that could only come from them.

Using AI to Nurture Creativity

We used ChatGPT to develop some prompts to help you consider how AI can nurture creativity and how we might teach this skill to our students.

1. AI as a Creative Thought Partner for Teachers ✎

📌 Goal: Use AI to **enhance lesson planning and creativity** in instruction.

- *Primary Prompt: "How can I use AI to generate lesson ideas, and then modify them to better fit my students' needs?"*
    - 🤔 **Follow-up:** *"What are three ways I could adapt an AI-generated lesson plan to make it more engaging and inquiry-based?"*
    - 💡 **Follow-up:** *"How do I ensure that AI-generated lesson ideas still reflect my students' unique interests, backgrounds, and learning needs?"*

Why this works: This keeps the **focus on teacher agency**—ensuring that AI serves as **a support tool rather than** the driving force of lesson design.

2. Helping Students Think with AI, Not Letting It Think for Them

Goal: Guide students to **critically engage** with AI rather than passively accept its responses.

- **Primary Prompt:** *"How can I model the process of improving AI-generated content to make it more thoughtful, creative, or personal?"*
  - **Follow-up:** *"How might students compare an AI-generated response to their own work and reflect on what makes theirs stronger?"*
  - *Follow-up: "What reflection questions can I give students to help them analyze AI's suggestions?"*

Why this works: Educators shift from viewing AI as a content generator to a tool for iterative thinking and deeper student engagement.

3. Designing Assignments That Encourage Iteration & Modification

Goal: Shift assignments from AI-friendly outputs to tasks requiring **student transformation.**

- **Primary Prompt:** *"How can I reframe a traditional assignment so that students must modify and personalize AI-generated content?"*
  - **Follow-up:** *"What specific instructions or scaffolds could I provide to ensure students go beyond AI's first response?"*
  - **Follow-up:** *"What are three ways I can design assignments where students combine multiple AI-generated ideas into something unique?"*

Why this works: This helps educators **stop thinking about preventing AI use** and instead **design assessments that reward originality, iteration, and synthesis.**

Anxiety

Many of us educators feel deeply anxious as we try to get to everything on our plate. Each school year begins with hope and excitement, but it also brings the reality of endless responsibilities and an ever-growing to-do list. When something new like AI is added to the plate, it can bring on even more anxiety. The thought of adapting to yet another change, managing concerns like cheating, and rethinking teaching strategies can feel overwhelming.

But while the idea of integrating AI into education may seem daunting, it's also an opportunity. Yes, AI challenges us to evaluate what we teach and how we teach it. In a world where AI can produce polished products in minutes, we must shift our thinking to reflect on what skills we want our students to develop without the help of a machine—and what skills and experiences the machine can enhance.

At first, this might create more anxiety. But when we reexamine hands-on activities, writing workshops, communication, collaboration, and rich discussions, we realize that these practices will benefit any student in an AI-enhanced world. Looking at this list, it's also clear that these are not just strategies for AI-proofing your classroom; they are good teaching practices. This allows us to pause, take a breath, and recognize that the foundation of what we do as educators is already strong and adaptable.

Of course, the anxiety isn't just about making time to adapt to AI; it's also about the weight of ensuring our students learn and thrive. To help ease this anxiety, we can ask ourselves, "How can AI be a partner in this work?" AI has the potential to break down barriers, make learning more accessible, and even lighten the administrative load that so often pulls us away from meaningful student interactions. Using AI to automate routine tasks, we free up time and energy to focus on what matters most: building relationships and fostering growth.

Jon

My favorite way to introduce new things in class: very quick and at the end. Why? I'm making it quick to keep frustration down and sense the energy of the kids' reactions. Why at the end? The bell will save me if it's all going bad!

Pausing, Reflecting, and Trusting Our Foundation

These prompts will help you use ChatGPT for reflection. They're perfect for engaging with a chatbot, so while you're reflecting, you're also practicing how to harness the power of a chatbot through conversation. This skill will transfer to all your chatbot interactions.

1. Recognizing Strengths & Stability

Goal: Use AI to reflect on what **already works** in teaching and remains true despite change.

- **Prompt:** *"Teaching has changed over time, but some core practices remain essential. What are the timeless elements of great teaching that have stayed effective across decades?"*
  - **Follow-up:** *"How can I ensure that any new tool I integrate supports rather than replaces these core teaching principles?"*
- **Prompt:** *"Help me reflect on my strengths as an educator. What are three ways I already create a meaningful learning experience for my students?"*
  - **Follow-up:** *"How can I use this reflection to stay grounded when facing educational shifts?"*

2. Seeing Change as an Evolution, Not a Disruption

Goal: Guide educators to see **how they have already adapted** and can continue to do so.

- **Prompt:** *"Education is always evolving. What are three major changes in teaching over the past twenty years, and how have teachers successfully adapted?"*
  - **Follow-up:** *"What are the common strategies educators have used to embrace these shifts while staying true to effective pedagogy?"*
- **Prompt:** *"I've adapted to many changes in my career. Can you help me list five ways I have already demonstrated resilience and adaptability in my teaching?"*

- **Follow-up:** *"What lessons can I take from my past experiences to help me feel confident about future innovations in education?"*

3. Trusting Pedagogy Over Tools

Goal: Help educators **reaffirm that great teaching is about pedagogy, not just technology**.

- **Prompt:** *"What are some high-impact teaching strategies that work with or without technology?"*
    - **Follow-up:** *"How can AI be used to enhance, rather than replace, these effective teaching strategies?"*
- **Prompt:** *"If I stripped away all technology, what are the essential elements of a great lesson?"*
    - **Follow-up:** *"How can I thoughtfully integrate AI to support, rather than overshadow, these elements?"*

Joy and EduProtocols

After riding the roller coaster of emotions AI stirs up for educators, we arrive at something often overlooked: joy. Beneath the worries, skepticism, and caution, there's a growing excitement about what generative AI can do *with* us, not *to* us. It's not just the thrill of new technology but AI's possibilities for reshaping our teaching and, ultimately, enriching students' lives.

At its core, teaching AI literacy is about giving students skills that go far beyond coding or technical know-how. We guide them to thoughtfully understand, question, and use this technology. The goal isn't to turn every student into a computer scientist; it's to give them agency over a tool that will undoubtedly shape their world. Teaching AI literacy lets us help them recognize ethical boundaries, think critically, and harness AI for creativity. This is teaching as empowerment, and there's joy in knowing we're preparing students to navigate the future with confidence. EduProtocols are the perfect partner for teaching AI literacy and keeping your joy.

What Are EduProtocols?

If you're new to EduProtocols, you might be wondering what they are, exactly. And more importantly, why people keep talking about them like they're the best thing since block scheduling.

EduProtocols are lesson frames. Think of them like containers you can pour your content into. You bring the standards and the content; the EduProtocol brings the structure, energy, and flow. They're short (usually ten to thirty-five minutes), repeatable, and ridiculously effective.

Repeatable is key. The magic of EduProtocols isn't in using them once; it's in using them again (and again). Repetition lowers students' cognitive load because they're not burning brainpower trying to figure out what they're supposed to do. That frees up their mental energy to actually focus on the learning.

Let me give you an example. My juniors love the Cyber Sandwich EduProtocol. The first time I introduced it, I had to walk them through all the steps: reading, annotating, partner talk, summary writing. But by the third or fourth round? They were practically running it themselves. I didn't even have to say anything. I just projected the prompt and let them get into it. That's the power of repetition and a clear lesson frame. They weren't confused or anxious. They were ready to learn.

EduProtocols aren't just efficient—they're fun. And, yes, I mean fun for teenagers. If I say, "We're doing a Fast and Curious," my students literally cheer. Why? These lessons are fast-paced, they're interactive, and they bring an element of joy and play. We're still hitting all the standards; we're just doing it in a way that doesn't suck the soul out of the room.

EduProtocols are built to support the Four Cs: communication, collaboration, critical thinking, and creativity. They're not just about remembering the definition of *synecdoche*. They're about making meaning together. Whether it's an Iron Chef lesson where students compare rhetorical appeals in Super Bowl ads or a Sketch and Tell on poetic devices, these protocols get students thinking, talking, and creating.

And because they're content-agnostic, you can use the same EduProtocol across multiple units and genres. I've used the same EduProtocols with poetry, nonfiction, research writing, and even grammar (don't tell my students—it didn't feel like grammar practice!). That's the beauty of the flexible lesson frames: I'm not reinventing the wheel, and my students aren't spinning in confusion. And once you've got your go-to EduProtocols in rotation, planning gets faster. And easier.

You might be thinking, "But will this work with my students?" Trust me, I've used EduProtocols with honors students, reluctant readers, and everyone in between. I've seen quiet students take the lead during Iron Chef and students who hate writing voluntarily revise during a Mini-Report. These lesson frames adapt to your learners, not the other way around.

And because the structure is familiar, you can build in feedback loops without breaking the flow. I've had students revise their responses mid-lesson, adjust their thinking during a partner discussion, or improve their summaries after a quick gallery walk. Feedback becomes a natural part of the rhythm, not one more thing to schedule.

If you want to get the full picture, definitely check out both volumes of *The EduProtocol Field Guide*. They're packed with ready-to-use lesson frames, real classroom examples, and tons of practical strategies to get started. These books are what first lit the spark for me while teaching online and in person at the same time, and I never looked back.

In this edition, we're showing you how to use EduProtocols to teach AI literacy, something every student (and teacher) needs right now. But here's the thing: These EduProtocols work in any content area. Whether you're teaching ancient civilizations, algebra, or art history, these lesson frames give you the structure to help your students develop the knowledge, skills, and mindsets to enable them to use AI safely, ethically, and effectively.

Our AI literacy EduProtocols are designed to scaffold these skills thoughtfully. Each EduProtocol is made to gradually build students' familiarity with AI's capabilities and limitations, allowing them to engage in ethical conversations about its use in ways that feel relevant to them. Through these structured experiences, they learn to see AI as a support for their creativity rather than a replacement.

The EduProtocols also invite teachers to bring real-world ethical issues into the classroom. With AI literacy at the forefront, students explore ethical and responsible AI use. They learn to ask questions like "How can I use AI in a way that aligns with my values?" and "When is it appropriate to rely on AI, and when should I approach a task independently?" Through guided activities and reflective practices embedded in our EduProtocols, students gain a deeper understanding of AI as a resource they can control rather than a tool that controls them.

For teachers, these EduProtocols mean more than just delivering content; they create opportunities to personalize learning and give students agency in meaningful ways. When students use AI to explore topics independently or collaborate on projects, teachers can guide them in applying critical thinking and ethical considerations. Our EduProtocols are crafted to make these interactions manageable, building confidence in teachers as they navigate this new terrain alongside their students. This approach allows us to reclaim joy in teaching by focusing on what matters most: fostering curiosity, creativity, and thoughtful exploration.

Finding Joy in AI

Try these prompts if you're struggling to see how AI might enhance our joy as educators!

1. Discovering AI as a Creative Spark 🎨

📌 Goal: Help educators see AI as a **source of inspiration and creativity** rather than just a tool for efficiency.

- **Prompt:** *"Surprise me! Give me five unexpected ways I could use AI to make my lessons more engaging."*
  - 🎭 **Follow-up:** *"Which of these ideas would be most fun for my students? How can I adapt it to fit my teaching style?"*
- **Prompt:** *"I love when students get excited about learning. How could AI help me design a lesson that sparks curiosity and wonder?"*
  - 🔍 **Follow-up:** *"Can you suggest a unique storytelling or role-play element that would make this lesson feel magical?"*

2. Using AI to Reignite Passion for Teaching ❤️

📌 Goal: Remind educators **why they love teaching** by using AI to reduce stress and bring **more joy into their work**.

- **Prompt:** *"Teaching brings me joy, but sometimes the workload is overwhelming. How can AI help me reclaim time for the parts of teaching I love most?"*
  - ⏳ **Follow-up:** *"Give me three specific AI strategies that could make grading, lesson planning, or communication more efficient without losing my personal touch."*
- **Prompt:** *"Write a fun and encouraging pep talk for a teacher who is feeling exhausted but still passionate about their work."*
  - 🌟 **Follow-up:** *"Now rewrite it as if it were delivered by an inspiring historical figure or fictional character!"*

3. Making AI Playful & Fun

Goal: Encourage **playfulness** with AI to reduce fear and make exploration enjoyable.

- **Prompt:** *"Let's play! Give me a humorous, over-the-top AI-generated excuse for why I haven't finished grading my students' papers."*
    - **Follow-up:** *"Now make it even more ridiculous by turning it into a mini adventure story."*
- **Prompt:** *"Help me create a fun AI-powered classroom activity that feels like a game rather than an assignment."*
    - **Follow-up:** *"How can I adapt this idea to fit different age groups or subjects?"*

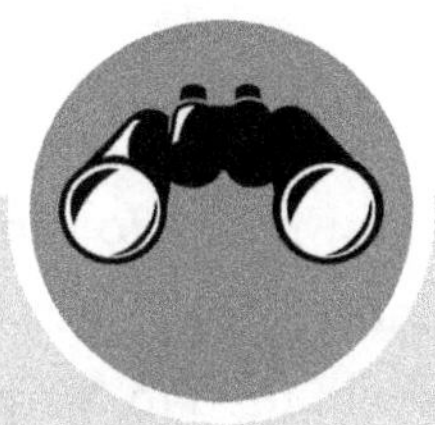

Chapter 3
Managing the Overwhelm: AI Smart Start for Educators

When I first discovered ChatGPT, I was amazed. There was an AI tool that could create essential questions for my classes, help me brainstorm lesson ideas, and even draft emails. It felt like I had stumbled upon a treasure chest of endless possibilities. I dove in headfirst, excited to see how this tool could transform my teaching.

But soon, my excitement gave way to a feeling of overwhelm. For every cool thing ChatGPT could do, ten other AI tools promised to revolutionize my classroom. There were AI graders, student progress trackers, slide deck creators, and image generators. I was adrift in an AI ocean, unsure which waves to ride.

I took a deep breath. If Smart Start worked for my students, maybe it could work for me, too.

I began with a list of what my students and I needed to know. Did I really need an AI tool that could predict when students would raise their hands? I laughed. No, I needed tools to enhance my teaching and save time. So, I focused on the essentials: an AI tool for giving feedback, one for creating engaging content, and one to improve my workflow.

As I started using these tools, I stressed less and focused more on what was important. The feedback tool helped me give more detailed feedback to my students much faster than I had ever been

Kate

What I love about EduProtocols is that you begin with a Smart Start: a rep or two of the EduProtocol that has a low cognitive load.

Jon

It's like a practice before the big game!

Marlena

If you are spending hours on tasks that a computer can do in minutes, the decision isn't hard. You're just wasting time.

Marlena

Don't feel like you have to learn *all* the AI tools this weekend. Pick one. Play with it. Let it *marinate*. The goal isn't to become a robot whisperer—it's to make space for more teaching magic.

able to do. The tool I used to create content allowed me to gamify my curriculum—something I had always wanted to try but had never done because of the time it took. The tool I used to increase my professional efficiency meant I could leave school at the end of the day and head home to my family.

Slowly but surely, the rest of the AI ocean began to calm. I had my essentials, and that was enough. I learned that it wasn't about navigating every single wave but about finding the right tools for what I faced at the moment.

Just as we guide our students through an EduProtocol Smart Start to set them up for success, you can use the same approach. Consider this book your toolkit for navigating the sea of AI options. The idea is simple: Manage your overwhelm by focusing on what's essential and starting small. Identify the core tools that will impact your teaching and your students' learning, and let go of the rest.

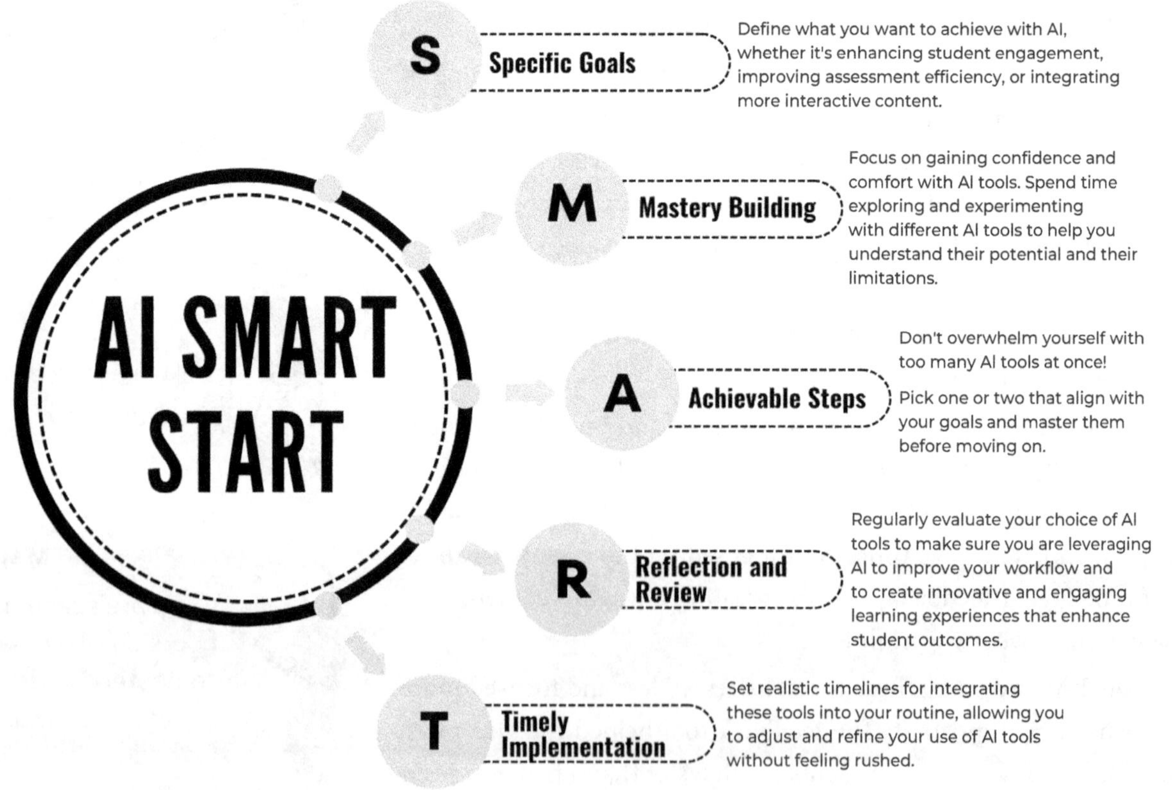

An AI Smart Start.

As I managed my own AI overwhelm in my practice, and as Nicole and I discussed AI in education further, one thing became clear: AI should never replace the human element of teaching. Look, we've all heard the nightmare scenario of AI taking over our classrooms and turning us into bystanders. That's not what we're aiming for. The secret sauce? Keeping the human in the loop. Sure, AI can grade papers faster than you can say "summer vacation," but it's our voice that brings the warmth, creativity, and understanding that make feedback valuable. By blending AI's superpowers with human intuition and care, we create a classroom that's not just smart but also connected. After all, no algorithm can replace a teacher's encouraging smile or a high five for a job well done!

Nicole

Also, if the tool doesn't work for you, put it back on the shelf—don't force it. Come back to it in a little bit. These tools are changing fast, and many are created by educators or with educator feedback, so they are catering to what we need.

Nicole and I talk about this all the time: If we don't keep the human side front and center, AI use stops being ethical. It's for that reason that we offer the acronym HUMAN to help us think about the ethical use of AI. Using this framework when interacting with AI can help you and your students use AI confidently and ethically.

Jon

Kids don't want generalized feedback from a robot—they want people to comment on the work. Never forget that the human element of teaching, regardless of platform, is the most crucial aspect!

That's why we've centered this book around HUMAN: to help you stay grounded, focused, and a little less overwhelmed.

Each section will also include two original AI literacy EduProtocols and one EduProtocol that you already know and love, all focused on AI literacy.

You don't need to use every EduProtocol for every step. Just grab the ones that fit your students and your content and use them often!

Feeling a little overwhelmed? That's okay—that means you're paying attention! But remember, you don't need to do *all the things*. You just need to start smart. Pick one tool. Try one EduProtocol. See what clicks for you and your students.

And here's a heads-up: AI tools change fast! While we offer suggestions for which AI tools you might want to integrate, we won't always tell you exactly what tool to use because what works today might be gone (or different) tomorrow. When it makes sense, we'll mention what we've used and liked. But in the end, finding the right tool is up to you. Think of this book as your guide for *how* to think about AI, not just *what* to use.

KEEP THE HUMAN IN THE LOOP

HALT

Halt and ask yourself...

- Is this something you want to use AI for?
- Is the outcome appropriate for the task?
- Is it an ethical use of AI?

UTILIZE

U

Utilize effective prompting.

- How might you utilize effective prompts to help craft your inquiry?
- What frameworks will help ensure the desired output?

MONITOR

M

Monitor for accuracy and bias.

- Do you have evidence to back up the information?
- What perspective is missing?
- Is the information presented neutrally or through a specific lens?

AUTHENTICATE

Authenticate through inquiry.

- Is it authentic for your voice or task?
- Is it my work or work that is appropriate to use?
- Does it enhance and not replace?

NOTE

N

Note key elements of usage.

- How did you use the AI?
- Did it help your thinking?
- Do you need to disclose that you used AI?
- Do you need to cite the AI?

Kate

Do you want to try a specific tool but don't know how to get started? Look on YouTube for tutorials (the companies that own the tools often have YouTube channels), look on social media groups (the companies also often have social media pages), or go to the tool's web page and see what PD is offered. There are often short courses you can watch that will get you up and running in no time!

So, take a deep breath, dive in, and let's get started!

You will find codes and TinyURLs throughout the book that take you to templates. You can also scan this QR code with your phone's default camera or visit tinyurl.com/ailiteracyedition to access all the templates in one place. It's important to note that the TinyURLs are case sensitive.

tinyurl.com/ailiteracyedition

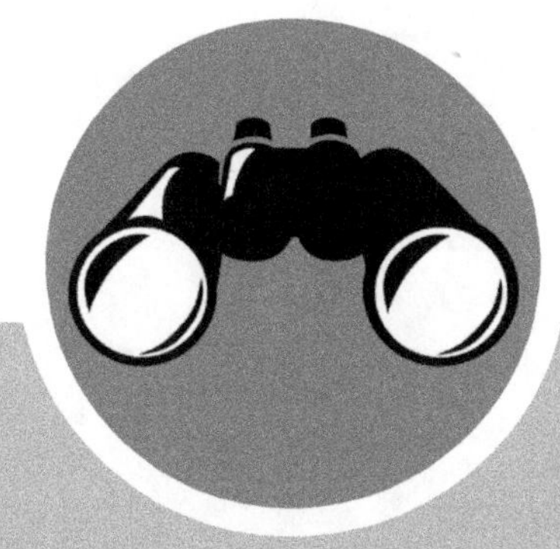

SECTION 2

Halt

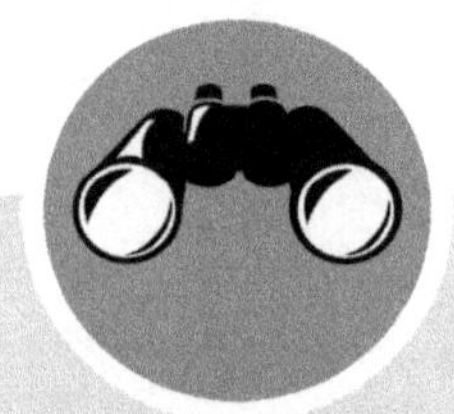

Chapter 4
HUMAN: Halt

It is interesting to see our reactions to AI and how it makes us pause in different ways. When I asked ChatGPT for a list of words for *halt*, it gave me words like *stop*, *pause*, *freeze*, *break*, *suspend*, *end*, *hold*, *interrupt*, *discontinue*, *delay*, *stand still*, *wait*, *block*, *obstruct*, *slow down*, and *postpone*. This initial list mirrors many of our gut reactions to AI: We might freeze, hesitate, or ban it. These responses are understandable as AI interrupts routines and changes traditional education methods. Although it's understandable, it's important that we don't remain stuck in this reaction.

What if we shift our perspective and approach *halt* with curiosity? When I asked ChatGPT for a list of words for *halt* focused on curiosity, the responses differed: *consider*, *reflect*, *evaluate*, *ponder*, *deliberate*, *analyze*, *reconsider*, *examine*, *review*, *question*, and *wonder*. This list has a different tone than our previous one and moves us forward thoughtfully and deliberately.

Kate

I did not practice halting at the beginning, either. But this perspective from two people who dove in and then realized there needs to be a pause can be helpful!

I wish I could say I approached AI thoughtfully and deliberately from the start. At first, I was full steam ahead, eager to share everything I'd discovered about AI with educators.

But my excitement soon met reality. After delivering a professional development session on AI, an educator reached out to ask if I could confirm whether AI wrote an email they'd received from their administrator who had been in this session. The email was meant to congratulate them on a job well done. As I read the email, I was excited to see that the information about prompting had stuck.

However, the educator's reaction was not one of excitement but disappointment. This was an aha moment for me, when I realized that when a genuine human connection is involved, we need to consider our use of artificial intelligence. This interaction was my first *halt* moment, and it made me realize that educators and their students need more than just technical knowledge of AI. We all need a framework to help us use it ethically and responsibly.

This is when Kate and I sat down and really started having conversations about keeping the human in the loop, and the HUMAN framework was born. Again, it's natural to view *halt* as a full stop or freeze, but what if we used our pause to consider and evaluate our intentions in using AI?

The *halt* part of HUMAN should happen at the beginning, middle, and end of your use of AI. Start by asking, "What specific goal am I aiming to achieve with AI? Is AI the best tool for this task, or could it be achieved through other means?" These questions help you decide whether AI is the right choice and whether it genuinely enhances what you're doing.

Consider how AI use aligns with human connection and authenticity. Does this task require a personal touch, and if so, will AI enhance or diminish that? Ask yourself, "How will using AI support my work rather than replace my expertise?" As you gain AI experience, you'll notice that some tasks benefit from its use while others do not. Monitor your use and continue to ask yourself these questions to avoid overreliance and allow AI to remain a tool rather than a crutch.

Throughout the process, revisit these questions to ensure your AI use aligns with your values. Once you reach a final output, evaluate whether the result and the method were ethically responsible. Part of this responsibility involves considering transparency: Is it important to disclose that AI was used in this work?

Another part of pausing to reflect is following the terms of service for these tools. Several tools are not for students' use, so you must read the terms of service and privacy policies before be-

Kate

I have found that using our halt EduProtocols with my students has led them to pause and do this thinking very naturally. My students want to use AI and are very concerned with using it ethically. Giving them the skills to halt before they dive in helps them gain the confidence to use AI tools to support their learning.

Marlena

Your first AI experiment doesn't have to be perfect—it just has to be curious. Think of it as a sandbox, not a test.

ginning. You should always check that the tools you use follow federal and state laws, the Family Educational Rights and Privacy Act (FERPA), the Children's Online Privacy Protection Rule (COPPA), and any policies your district may have around AI or technology use.

As you explore AI, let the HUMAN framework guide your journey. Start by halting—not to freeze but to thoughtfully and purposefully engage AI with curiosity and intention. The EduProtocols we'll cover in the following chapters—Bot Plot, AI Master Chef, and Worst Preso Ever: Joyful Disaster Remix—will help you and your students slow down, halt, and make informed decisions about your ethical and responsible use of AI.

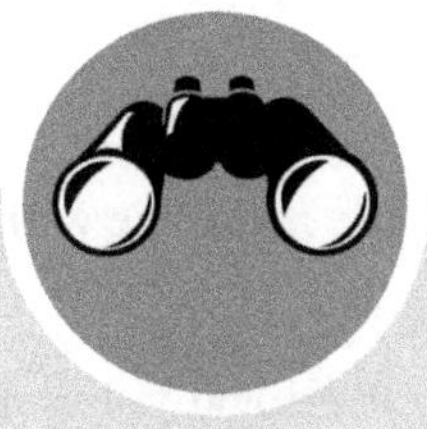

Chapter 5
The Bot Plot

The moment I mentioned AI, I could see my students tense up. They folded their arms and glanced sideways, like they were bracing for a lecture on plagiarism and cheating.

"So . . . are we allowed to use AI or not?" one student finally asked.

Before I could answer, another jumped in. "I heard it's basically the same as copying and pasting from the internet."

"Yeah, some teachers say AI is just a lazy way to avoid thinking."

There it was, the hesitation, the skepticism, the fear of doing something wrong. They had spent months hearing warnings about AI, how it was a slippery slope to academic dishonesty, how teachers were cracking down, and how it was safer to avoid it altogether. No wonder they were reluctant to have the conversation.

The truth is that AI isn't inherently good or bad. Like any tool, it all comes down to how we use it. So, instead of giving them a list of rules, I handed them the debate itself: the Bot Plot EduProtocol.

Instead of examining their own AI habits, students analyzed fictional scenarios—realistic but comfortably detached from their personal experiences. One by one, they ranked these scenarios on a continuum, ranging from completely unacceptable to totally fine, defending their reasoning along the way. And trust me, those conversations were never simple.

"Wait, what if they only used AI to brainstorm? That's not really cheating, is it?"

Marlena

We can't just hand students AI tools and hope for the best. We've got to model the messy thinking and make space for the tough conversations.

Nicole

Kate uses these scenarios and conversations in her classroom, but we need to discuss them at all levels of education. Talking about how AI can be used ethically eases educators' minds, too, and helps us analyze how we want to use it.

"Yeah, but what if they just copied the whole response without changing anything?"

"What if they thought they were using it ethically, but they didn't realize they were making a mistake?"

Before long, they weren't just talking about AI anymore. They were digging deeper, questioning assumptions, and wrestling with all the gray areas.

The best part? This discussion serves as our *foundation* for utilizing AI in the classroom. When questions arise—"Can I use AI for this?" or "Where's the line?"—we go back to the scenarios, using them as a shared reference point. Instead of me handing down rules, we build our understanding *together*. AI doesn't have to be something to fear or avoid. With the right conversation, it becomes a tool we learn to use thoughtfully, as co-learners.

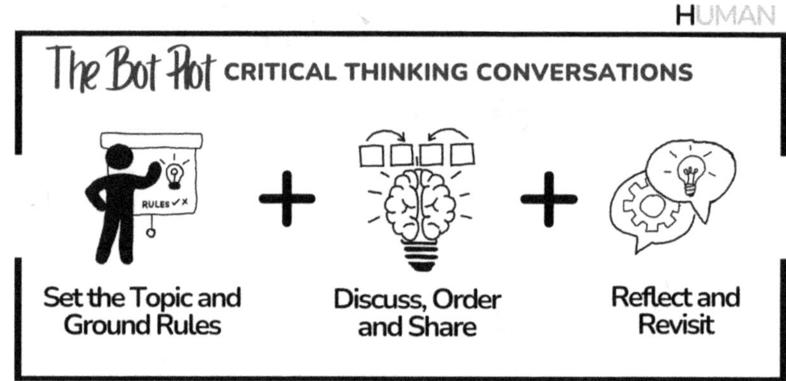

Description

This EduProtocol helps students engage in structured conversations about complex topics, fostering critical thinking, respectful communication, and exploration of multiple viewpoints. The conversations have no predetermined outcome, encouraging students to explore ideas along a continuum, moving from surface-level awareness to deeper reflection.

Academic Goals

- Students will understand how to use AI ethically.
- The class will discuss clear expectations about AI use in the classroom.
- We will keep the HUMAN in AI. This EduProtocol builds skills around the *H* (halt) in HUMAN.

Teacher Big Ideas

- This EduProtocol generates a shared understanding of ethical AI use in the classroom.

Prepare for the Activity

1. Decide on your topic for the continuum (in this case, we're focusing on general ethical AI use in the classroom).
2. Gather or create your initial set of scenarios. You can write your own or use the ones we have provided for this activity.
3. Open the Bot Plot template and make a copy for your class. Preload your scenarios if you have written your own.

The Activity

Step 1: Set the Topic and Ground Rules

- The teacher sets the topic and introduces the concept of a continuum (a spectrum of ideas or opinions without one "right" answer). This may only be necessary the first time you introduce this EduProtocol.
- Establish ground rules for respectful communication and active listening:
  - Listen to understand, not to respond.
  - Speak one at a time and allow others to share.

tinyurl.com/botplotAI

- Disagree respectfully by focusing on the idea, not the person.
- Build on others' ideas.

Step 2: Discuss and Order

1. Scan the QR code or visit tinyurl.com/botplotAI to access the Bot Plot template.
2. Provide students with the template of scenarios.
3. In small groups, have students discuss and categorize each scenario from "Unacceptable AI Use" to "Acceptable AI Use."

Amari has been assigned a creative writing project. She uses an AI tool to generate a list of unique story ideas and then picks one that inspires her. She writes the story herself, based on the AI-generated idea.

James was running out of time to complete his history assignment. He copied the prompt into an AI tool and let it generate a full answer. He submits the response without making any changes or edits.

Mia writes a persuasive essay on environmental issues and uses an AI tool to suggest grammar and style edits. She reviews each suggestion, choosing which ones she agrees with and ignoring others.

Alex struggles with reading comprehension, so they paste a challenging science article into an AI tool to get a simpler version of the text. They then use this summary to understand the content better before answering questions in their own words.

Olivia has multiple assignments due. To manage her workload, she uses an AI tool to summarize a reading assignment so she can quickly complete the reading response. She submits her response, using the AI summary without reading the full text.

Acceptable AI Use — Unacceptable AI Use

Tara is assigned a worksheet of algebra problems for homework. She uses AI to solve a few examples as a guide but completes the rest on her own, using what she learned from the AI's examples.

Isabel writes an essay and then asks an AI tool to enhance her writing by suggesting more sophisticated vocabulary and complex sentence structures. She accepts all suggestions, resulting in a final product that is significantly altered from her original draft.

Lily finishes her math homework and uses an AI tool to check her answers. If she gets something wrong, she has the AI explain the mistake to her before she reattempts the problem.

Samir is researching for his history essay. He uses an AI tool to find reputable sources and asks it questions about his topic. He still reads the articles himself and writes his essay based on his understanding of the sources.

Charlie is writing an essay as part of their college application process. They ask an AI tool to write a draft for them, giving it details about their experience. They then make small edits and submit it as their own work.

Load the Bot Plot scenarios in Google Slides, or check out the interactive capabilities in Genially for this activity.

Step 3: Add Scenarios

1. After students have discussed each scenario and placed it on the continuum, have them write two of their own scenarios about using AI in a classroom.

2. Have small groups trade scenarios. Groups will add these two student-generated scenarios to their continuum using the blank shapes. Then, have the small groups discuss and place these new student-generated scenarios on their continuum.

Step 4: Share and Discuss

1. Each group completes the Bot Plot template and adds it to a shared slide deck. It's okay to set a time limit for this; it should be fast because the thinking is already done. The groups then share their scenarios and slides.
2. Discuss the results as a class. How does this help us understand or agree on how we should use AI in the classroom? If your school has an AI use policy or an academic honesty policy, you might also discuss how this informs that policy. Or you could discuss how this can be used in the creation of a policy.

Scenario One	Scenario Two
Placement on Continuum	Placement on Continuum
Rationale	Rationale

The Bot Plot individual slide template.

Kate

I like to do this reflection using the Thin Slides EduProtocol. This is a great way for teachers to share their thoughts, too. Join in on the Thin Slides!

Jon

Bot Plot is like a Thin Prompt!

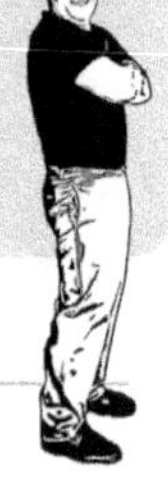

Step 5: Reflect and Revisit

1. Ask students, "After this discussion, where do you stand on AI use in the classroom?"
2. Students share their reflections.

Suggestions for Teachers

- Use this EduProtocol to look at ethical AI usage in relation to any topic, from technology to history to current events.
- Modify it for formal or informal discussions. In informal conversations, simplify the structure; for formal ones, explore each continuum point more deeply.
- Teachers can use AI to brainstorm scenarios or discussion prompts (e.g., "Generate three ethical dilemmas about AI use in the classroom").
- If appropriate, students can use AI to generate alternative scenarios for the continuum.

EduProtocol AI Power-Up: Integrating AI

Want to take the Bot Plot EduProtocol to the next level? Try hosting it in Curipod, an interactive slide-based platform that lets students engage in real-time discussion, ranking, and collaboration. Or try SchoolAI, where you can create a space for students to discuss their reasoning with a customized chatbot.

With Curipod you can:

- Create a drag-and-drop continuum where students place scenarios from "Unacceptable AI Use" to "Acceptable AI Use."
- Add AI-generated scenario prompts using Curipod's built-in generative tool or copy/paste your own.
- Facilitate live-group discussions or asynchronous responses that allow students to justify the placements they chose and react to others.

- Revisit the continuum later in the unit to see how students' thinking evolves.

With SchoolAI you can:

- Create a custom chatbot persona, like a confused classmate or a skeptical teacher, that challenges students to explain their thinking clearly and with evidence.
- Scaffold critical reasoning with preprogrammed guiding questions to help students uncover bias, consider consequences, or propose improvements.

Using AI to power up this EduProtocol will help students feel more ownership over the conversation and encourage deep reasoning without the pressure of a traditional debate.

Leverage AI to Apply to Your Content

Bot Plot works especially well for AI ethics because it makes the conversation concrete. Rather than asking students if AI is cheating, you give them realistic snapshots of student choices, and then you ask them to decide where those belong on the continuum and explain why. AI can generate these scenarios fast, but the learning comes from what students do next: They notice patterns, debate the gray areas, reference classroom norms, and refine their thinking about responsible AI use. These scenarios are designed to feel like a real high school classroom, so students can practice making good decisions before the stakes are high. We've created scenarios for different content areas below. If you don't see what you need, try the prompt at the end in your favorite large language model (LLM), such as ChatGPT, Claude, Gemini, MagicSchool's Raina, and create your own!

ELA

- Maya wrote a paragraph and used AI to suggest two revision moves, then rewrote the paragraph in her own words.
- Jake asked AI to brainstorm possible thesis statements, chose one, and revised it to match his actual evidence.

- Priya pasted a quote and asked AI, "What might this quote suggest?" Then she used the idea without reading the rest of the chapter.
- Emma asked AI to rewrite her whole essay and submitted it after changing a few words.
- Jordan used AI to check whether the paragraph includes more summary or analysis, then added original commentary.
- Kevin asked AI for better vocabulary and replaced words without understanding them.
- Aaliyah used AI to create a works cited section and copied it without verifying any sources.

Social Studies/History

- Omar summarized a source in their own words, then used AI to check what might be missing and verified against the original.
- Sofia used AI to generate counterclaims to her argument, then chose one and found evidence in class-approved sources.
- Ben asked AI to give him five citations and added them to the bibliography without checking whether they existed.
- Natalie used AI to rewrite a paragraph to sound more formal but kept the same evidence and ideas.
- Alex asked AI to explain an event and repeated the explanation even though it conflicted with class materials.
- Zoe used AI to identify possible bias in a source, then used a sourcing checklist to confirm.
- Hassan asked AI to write a speech in the voice of a historical figure and presented it as if it were historically accurate.

Science

- Grace wrote a lab conclusion and used AI to suggest possible sources of error, then kept only the ones that matched her actual procedure and data.
- Diego asked AI to turn his notes into study questions, then answered them and checked misunderstandings using class resources.
- Lily's results didn't match expectations, so Lily asked AI to invent "realistic" data to make the graph look better.
- Ethan used AI to generate a graph from their data but wrote the interpretation independently.
- Hannah asked AI for an explanation, then fact-checked the key claims using the textbook and notes before using it.
- Minh asked AI to write the conclusion so it would "sound scientific" and copied it without understanding it.
- Sara left out a safety mistake that happened during the lab and asked AI how to write the report so it wouldn't "look bad."

Math

- Ryan solved the problems, then used AI to check answers and point out the first mistake, and he corrected the work.
- Mei asked AI for a hint only ("Don't solve it, tell me the next step and why"), then finished independently.
- Connor pasted the problem into AI and copied the full solution steps into the homework.
- Ava used AI to generate two similar practice problems and tried them before checking the answers.
- Kenji asked AI to explain a method and used it even though Kenji couldn't explain why it works.
- Leila used AI to create a word problem, and the scenario included unrealistic assumptions, so she revised it to fit real constraints.

- Marcus changed a few numbers in a dataset and asked AI to recalculate so the class survey would "look cleaner."

Visual Arts/Music

- Ella used AI to brainstorm ten composition ideas, chose one, and created the final piece independently.
- Tyler used AI to generate a reference image and credited it, then drew the artwork from scratch.
- Julie submitted an AI-generated image as the final artwork without disclosure.
- Nina asked AI to write an artist statement, then rewrote it in her voice with specific details from the process.
- Liam asked AI to imitate a living artist's exact style and submitted it as "inspired by" without discussion.
- Jasmine used AI to generate critique sentence starters and used them in peer feedback.
- Caleb used AI to generate lyrics and turned them in as original writing.

Computer Science/Digital Literacy

- Arjun used AI to explain an error message in plain language, then he chose what to change and documented the fix.
- Emily asked AI to debug code and pasted the fix without understanding what changed.
- Chris used AI to generate test cases, ran them, and improved the program based on the results.
- Brianna asked AI to write the entire program and submitted it as her work.
- Dylan used AI to draft documentation, then revised it to match how the program actually works.
- Elena asked AI for two algorithm options, compared trade-offs, and chose one with justification.

- Noah used AI for a project idea and included personal data in the prompt.

Wood/Metal Shop

- Sam used AI to generate a step-by-step build plan, then checked it against shop rules and revised it with the teacher.
- Maria asked AI for tool recommendations and followed them without confirming safety requirements or proper PPE.
- Jason used AI to create a cut list, then double-checked measurements and material constraints before cutting.
- Logan used AI to write the reflection, but the reflection didn't match what Logan actually built or struggled with.
- Tessa used AI to brainstorm joinery options, then chose one and explained why it fit the project goals.
- Malik asked AI how to hide a mistake in the project so it would "pass inspection."
- Chloe used AI to estimate cost and waste, then revised the design to be more efficient.

Foods

- Aiden used AI to generate recipe variations based on time, budget, and dietary needs, then tested and adjusted based on the results.
- Camila used AI to scale a recipe and checked the math before cooking.
- Nick used AI to write a nutrition analysis and reported it as fact without verifying.
- Sabrina asked AI for a substitution, then researched whether it would work for texture and food safety.
- Eli used AI to plan a meal but ignored allergen guidance and didn't check ingredient labels.

- Hailey used AI to write the lab report/reflection and rewrote it to include specific details about technique and outcomes.
- DeShawn asked AI to make the final product sound "healthy" even though the ingredient list didn't match.

Advisory/Life Skills

- Olivia drafted an email to a teacher and used AI to polish tone while keeping the message honest and specific.
- Jayden used AI to role-play a hard conversation, then reflected on what sounded respectful and what didn't.
- Valerie asked AI to write a personal reflection and submitted it even though it didn't sound like her.
- Brandon asked AI for coping strategies, then chose two and made a realistic plan to try them that week.
- Riley shared private information in an AI prompt without realizing it could be stored.
- Aaron used AI to create a weekly schedule, then revised it to fit real commitments and sleep needs.
- Madison used AI to generate excuses for missing work.

Prompt (for All Subject Areas)

Create six to eight short classroom scenarios written like this: "A student did ____ and used AI to ____." Make them realistic for [high/middle] school. Include a mix of clearly acceptable uses of AI in the classroom, gray areas, and clearly inappropriate uses. Keep each scenario to one to two sentences. Avoid big content themes; focus on the work process and decision point.

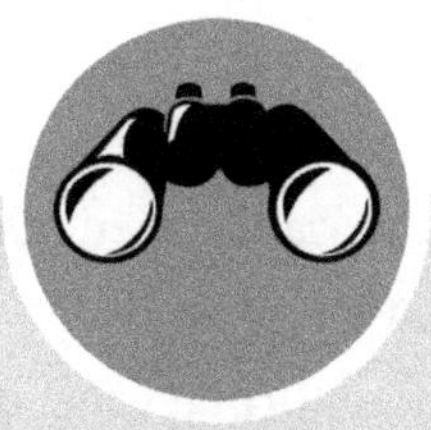

Chapter 6
AI Master Chef

It starts with skepticism. I can see it in their faces, the way they lean back in their chairs, eyes flicking toward their friends as if to say, "Is she serious? We're using AI in English class?"

"All right," I say, pulling up MagicStudent on the projector. "Let's see what it can do."

A few students raise their eyebrows. One mutters, "Isn't that cheating?"

"Good question," I say, stepping closer. "And that's exactly why we're talking about it. It's not going away. You're going to need to know how to use it ethically. So let's experiment."

I go through the tools I have deployed to them: a writing feedback generator, a step-by-step tool that will give directions for any task, and a tool that will help them get examples of how to use literary devices to enhance their writing. I then show them how this platform protects their data and privacy and how it doesn't require an email login to access it. They look willing to try it out.

"Wait, it can do all that?"

"Well, let's try. I invite you to put in all or part of your draft of your 'Perfect First Page.'" This is a short memoir piece that we have been drafting for a couple of days. "Pick one of the tools and see what it can do."

Silence. Then: "Whoa."

A few students sit up straighter. One leans forward. Another whispers, "That's actually kinda cool."

I smile. "Right? But here's the thing—does AI always get it right?"

They scan the output on their screen. "Mine said I needed better sentence variety, but I know I've done that well!" says one student. Another points out that it suggests a more formal tone, even though this piece is meant to be informal.

They aren't just accepting the technology; they are thinking critically about it.

Then comes the real aha moment.

"So . . . we're not just letting AI do the work?" one student asks slowly. "We're, like, collaborating with it?"

I smile. "Exactly. You're the writer. AI is just another tool in your toolkit. It can help, but it can't replace you. It doesn't have your ideas, your experiences, your voice. It's up to you to evaluate the feedback and decide what to do with it. You don't have to take it just because a robot suggests it. It's your writing."

Marlena

Just because AI suggests it doesn't mean it's right! That moment when students push back, that's the magic!

Nods all around. A few students immediately return to their laptops, eager to test things out. I hear one whisper, "This is kinda fun."

That's when I know: They get it. The fear and skepticism have cracked open, making space for curiosity. And in that moment, I'm not just teaching English. I'm teaching them how to navigate a future where AI isn't the enemy but an ally in their creative process. And most importantly, they are in control; they make all the final decisions.

This EduProtocol will help you show your students the importance of halting before they use AI output. They will keep the human in the loop by evaluating the feedback and then making all the final decisions using their human ability of discernment.

HUMAN

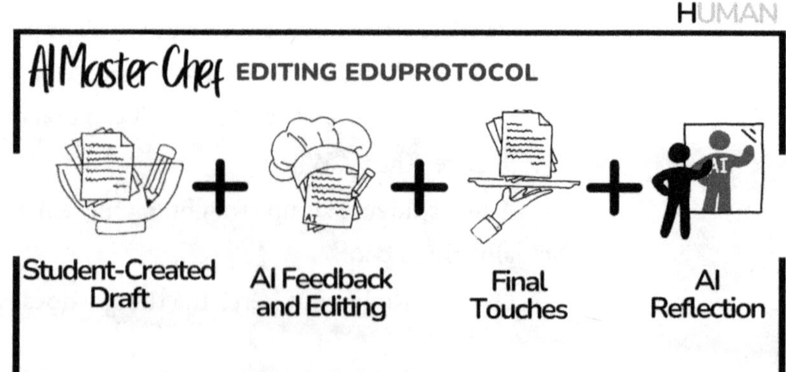

Description

In this EduProtocol, students act as master chefs of their writing. They draft original work first, then use AI as a sous-chef to suggest technical improvements like grammar, clarity, and tone. But students remain in full control of creative and stylistic choices. The goal is to build critical thinking and discernment: Students learn to evaluate AI feedback, decide what to keep or reject, and maintain their own voice throughout the process.

Kate

There are numerous platforms available for schools, equipped with safety features. My favorites at the moment are MagicSchool, Snorkl, and SchoolAI. These platforms have feedback tools already built in, so students won't have to be proficient at prompting to receive good feedback.

Academic Goals

- Students will understand how to use AI as a partner and not rely on it.
- The class will discuss clear expectations around AI use in the classroom.
- We will keep the HUMAN in AI. This EduProtocol builds skills around the *H* (halt) in HUMAN.

Teacher Big Ideas

- This EduProtocol models using AI as a partner.
- This EduProtocol starts to develop a conversation around how AI might be used in the classroom.

*tinyurl.com/*aimasterchef

Prepare for the Activity

1. Select or assign a writing task that will be used with this EduProtocol (narrative, analysis, reflection, lab report, etc.). Ensure students have written this first draft without AI assistance.
2. Choose the AI tool(s) students will use for feedback.
3. Prepare the template. (Scan the QR code or visit tinyurl.com/aimasterchef to access the AI Master Chef template.)

Kate

Plan to model the activity for the students. Show them how to use the AI tool you selected.

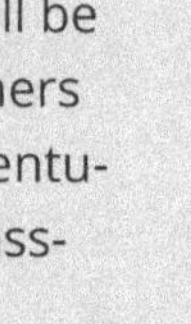

Kate

You do not have to be an expert on the tool! Learn what you can and let your students help you figure out the rest. They will be happy to be co-learners with you and will eventually become your classroom experts!

Jon

Every single new tech I've ever used in class has been heavily influenced by student comments and ideas from the first few uses—make sure to listen to your co-testers!

The Activity

Step 1: Preparation

Students write their initial drafts without AI to ensure creativity and original thinking.

Step 2: Feedback and Editing

- Students consult AI tools using prompts to elicit:
    - Suggestions for sentence structure, grammar, and spelling.
    - Feedback on clarity, tone, and conciseness.
- Remember, AI is the assistant, not the chef. Students—the head chefs—make every final decision.

Step 3: Final Touches

1. Students perform a final self-edit without AI to make personal stylistic changes and ensure their voice shines through.

Which ingredients did you choose?

*Remember, you're the chef!

Choose four AI edits: two you used, two you rejected, and why.

AI Suggestion:	Did you use it? If yes, show your revised sentence(s):	Why did you use or reject this AI suggestion?

AI Master Chef students evaluate the changes in their writing.

2. They also confirm that the content stays true to their original intent and purpose.
3. Students evaluate their changes with the template, recording a few of the changes they chose to keep and reject.

Step 4: Disclosure

- Students write a brief note on their assignment about how AI contributed to their work. Example: "I used AI to suggest grammar improvements and generate feedback on sentence clarity."
- Have students reflect on their AI use and answer these additional AI Master Chef template questions:
  - What did AI help you learn about your writing?
  - What did you notice about the suggestions you rejected or kept?
  - What will you do differently in your next draft?
- These parts of the activity may take place over several days.

Kate

Don't be afraid to use AI to help you create prompts to share with students. Utilizing AI to create prompts often generates helpful suggestions. Try prompting your AI with something like this: "I'd like to provide my students with some prompts to use for feedback with an AI tool. What are some prompts I can give them that will help them with their diction, sentence variety, and grammar?" (Or ask for whatever skills your students are working on!) Remember to use AI to customize these prompts for your students and the assignment.

Reflect

*Remember, you're the chef!

What did AI help you learn about your writing?	What did you notice about the suggestions you rejected or kept?	What will you do differently in your next draft?

Have students reflect on their AI use with this template.

Nicole

How to take feedback is not always a skill we think to teach students, but we are often frustrated when they don't respond or know how to use it. It's a skill, just like writing, and students need explicit instruction on how to interpret it, understand whether it's useful, and decide whether to accept or reject it. This gives students the power to stay in control of their work, strengthen their voice, and build critical thinking and confidence.

Suggestions for Teachers

- If you're worried about students' overreliance on AI, try giving limits:
    - Limit their interactions to only twice per draft.
    - Students must reject at least three AI suggestions and explain why.
- Guide students through the process of using the AI feedback. Model how it's done in front of the class or provide a decision framework such as SIMMER.

Decision Framework: When to Use AI or Your Own Skills?

Use the S.I.M.M.E.R. Checklist before and during the editing process:

Syntax – Is AI suggesting correct grammar changes? → If the sentence flows naturally, trust your judgment.

Intent – Does the change align with what you want to say? → If AI's suggestion alters your meaning, modify it yourself.

Meaning – Is your message clear, or is AI improving clarity? → If AI helps with clarity, use it. If not, rephrase in your voice.

Mechanics – Are AI's suggestions limited to technical corrections? → Use AI for punctuation and spelling but review all changes yourself.

Engagement – Is your writing still engaging and unique? → If AI makes your writing sound robotic, rework it manually.

Reflection – Did you learn from AI's feedback? → Use feedback as a learning moment to improve future writing.

EduProtocol AI Power-Up: Integrating AI

Ready to supercharge AI Master Chef? Pair this EduProtocol with Snorkl, a tool that helps students identify, explain, and transfer knowledge, or MagicSchool's MagicStudent, which gives targeted, student-friendly feedback to help polish the final dish.

Here's how Snorkl brings flavor to this EduProtocol:

- Snorkl gives students two to three focused suggestions at a time—no walls of AI text, just actionable insights tied to specific learning goals.
- Because Snorkl's feedback is suggestion-based (not rewrite-based), students have to decide: Keep it? Tweak it? Toss it? That decision-making process is the heart of AI Master Chef. Have students use this EduProtocol to analyze Snorkl's feedback.

Here's how MagicStudent can add spice to this EduProtocol:

- It provides feedback on drafts of students' AI Master Chef creations, focusing on clarity, structure, creativity, and tone.
- It highlights specific revision opportunities such as vague language, missing evidence, or weak transitions.
- It offers reflection prompts to help students think through their creative choices.

With AI as their sous-chef, students stay in charge of their final dish!

Leverage AI to Apply to Your Content

This EduProtocol works across all content areas where students write to express their ideas, whether explaining a process, constructing an argument, reflecting on learning, or analyzing a topic.

Students draft their work first, then use AI tools to refine grammar, clarity, and tone while owning the content, voice, and final editorial decisions. The goal is to help students strengthen their writing and critical thinking without relying on AI or allowing it to shape their ideas.

Chapter 7

Worst Preso Ever: Joyful Disaster Remix

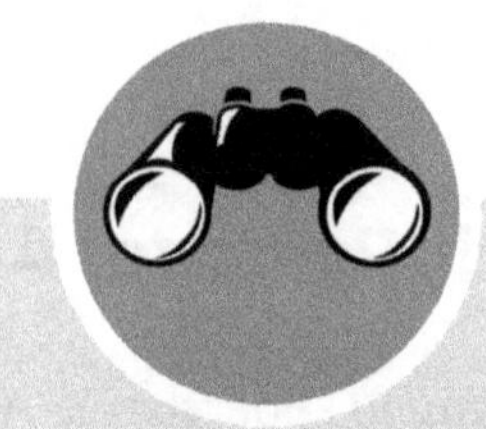

There's a special kind of exhaustion that only a teacher who has sat through twenty-seven student presentations in one day can understand. It's not just the fatigue of watching the same Canva template used (badly) over and over. It's the visual assault that starts around slide 7 of presentation 14, when someone's design choices make you want to throw your laptop across the room.

One day, midway through presentations, I sat in the back of my classroom, pretending my coffee wasn't empty. The slide on the screen featured bright yellow text on a white background, a pixelated GIF of a cat doing Fortnite dances, and a font I'm almost positive was called Bloody Vampire. My eyes were bleeding.

It was the moment I knew I needed something different. Something that would let students playfully fail forward, explore the wrong way to present, and then reflect on what made it so bad. I also knew it was the perfect opportunity to sneak in a refresher on ethical AI use since we had been discussing it for about nine weeks.

So I invented Worst Preso Ever: Joyful Disaster Remix. Based on the classic Worst Preso Ever EduProtocol, this version is all about intentionally making bad design choices, both in terms of design and AI use. Students are challenged to create over-the-top, misguided, laughably awful AI-infused presentations. And then they present someone else's mess. This one is best done after students are clear on the ethical and responsible use of AI; they must know the rules before they can break them.

It's chaos. It's hilarious. And it's the perfect way to reinforce how to halt.

In the pages ahead, we'll walk you through exactly how to run this EduProtocol, including setup, presentation instructions, debrief ideas, and reflection prompts. It's fast-paced, student-centered, and rooted in critical thinking. This EduProtocol will help students build one of the most important habits they will need when working with AI: pause first. Ask the hard questions. Choose tools with intention.

Description

In Worst Preso Ever: Joyful Disaster Remix, students intentionally create poorly designed, ethically questionable presentations that showcase the wrong ways to use design and AI.

Working in groups, they build a slide deck that includes bad design choices (such as hard-to-read fonts, clashing colors, or excessive GIFs) alongside examples of poor AI use (such as relying on AI or showing a lack of transparency).

The twist: Students will not present their own slides. They will present another group's slide deck, adding humor and distance

Nicole

This activity is not only valuable for students but also for adults. I've observed many classrooms and professional development sessions where the facilitator struggled with basic presentation design elements, such as visual clarity, consistency, and layout. While not as extreme as some student examples, the issues are still noticeable. With that in mind, I encourage you to complete the Worst Preso activity yourself. Afterward, take part in Worst Preso Ever: Joyful Disaster Remix. Both experiences offer meaningful learning opportunities; I've gained a great deal from them myself, and I've seen many adults do the same.

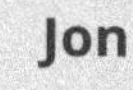

Jon

Nothing I've ever created has generated the pure, joyful laughter that comes with a class session of Worst Preso Ever. So glad this adaptation is in here!

while deepening their understanding of how bad choices, both visual and ethical, can affect an audience. This is a joyful, high-energy EduProtocol.

Cover slide to the slide deck Kate gave her students. The background is yellow, and the font is red. It features three unrelated GIFs and a random aardvark image. There are misspellings. It's bad.

Academic Goals

- Students will build critical thinking skills and practice intentional reflection on ethical and responsible AI use.
- The class will develop awareness of how poor design and unethical AI use affect the audience's experience.
- Learners will strengthen presentation and speaking skills through playful, low-stakes practice.

Marlena

If you hear snort-laughing in the middle of the presentations, fear not! That's the sound of joyful disaster *and* deep learning at the same time!

Teacher Big Ideas

- Students need opportunities to explore both the positive and negative uses of AI in a safe, low-stakes environment.
- Humor and intentional failure can be powerful tools for learning.
- The halt mindset is a habit that develops through repeated, authentic practice, not a one-time lesson.

Kate

Get ready, because after doing this EduProtocol, your students might consider themselves presentation connoisseurs. They will absolutely start critiquing your slides, too. Just smile and tell them it's evidence of learning. (Then go fix your fonts!)

Prepare for the Activity

1. Plan for one-to-one devices.
2. Find and bookmark the video "Life After Death by PowerPoint" by Don McMillan on YouTube.
3. Make the basic template in the platform of your choice.
4. Show students how to start building their slide deck.

The Activity

Step 1: Introduce the Rules for Creating Presentations

- Show students the YouTube video "Life After Death by PowerPoint" by Don McMillan.
- As you show the video, pause after each "no, no" and allow students time to take notes on what they should not do. The video covers key tips such as avoiding too many bullet points, limiting data on a slide, and considering animation versus effectiveness.

Step 2: Create the Slide Deck

1. Form groups of five students.

2. Each student builds one slide per rule broken, featuring bad use of AI and labeling each error. Keep it fun and moving along so that students stay engaged.
3. Help students understand that you're looking for effort and that they're expected to work for the entire time allotted (approximately ten minutes—they're each only building one slide, so it should be fast!).

Summary of Build Task for Students

AI Connection	Break One Rule per Slide	Five per Deck	Connect
Students come up with one bad use of AI per slide.	The goal is to highlight the errors—too many broken rules on a slide creates a jumbled mess!	Break a total of five rules per student deck.	List the rule being broken on the slide.

Step 3: Present with a Twist

Don't tell students ahead of time, but they will be presenting another group's slide deck. This exchange adds a layer of fun to the activity and makes it hilarious for everyone. However, in the moment of chaotic fun, the students begin to understand and appreciate the wrongness, which allows them to see the rightness.

Step 4: Debrief

- After all presentations are complete, guide students through a quick debrief. The goal is to help them reflect on what made the slides ineffective or unethical and how halt thinking could improve future AI use. You can do this as a whole-class discussion, small-group share-out, quickwrite, or exit ticket.
- Possible debrief questions:
  - What made these presentations "the worst"?
  - Where did poor AI use show up?

- What halt questions were clearly ignored?
- When is AI helpful? When is it a crutch?
- What choices (design or ethical) would you make differently next time?

Step 5: Optional Extension

Have students choose one AI-related misuse from another group and fix it by applying halt, either as a written reflection or as a revised slide.

Suggestions for Teachers

- This EduProtocol works best after students have had experience with ethical AI use. It's a remix, not an introduction, so be sure they've already wrestled with the core HUMAN framework questions.
- Keep it moving, keep it light. The tempo matters. Presentations should be fast, funny, and focused. Embrace the chaos, but steer it just enough to keep students engaged and on task.

KEEP THE HUMAN IN THE LOOP

HALT

Halt and ask yourself...

- Is this something you want to use AI for?
- Is the outcome appropriate for the task?
- Is it an ethical use of AI?

UTILIZE

Utilize effective prompting.

- How might you utilize effective prompts to help craft your inquiry?
- What frameworks will help ensure the desired output?

MONITOR

Monitor for accuracy and bias.

- Do you have evidence to back up the information?
- What perspective is missing?
- Is the information presented neutrally or through a specific lens?

AUTHENTICATE

Authenticate through inquiry.

- Is it authentic for your voice or task?
- Is it my work or work that is appropriate to use?
- Does it enhance and not replace?

NOTE

Note key elements of usage.

- How did you use the AI?
- Did it help your thinking?
- Do you need to disclose that you used AI?
- Do you need to cite the AI?

- Celebrate the best of the worst. End with lighthearted awards like Most Ethically Questionable AI Use, Cringiest Slides, or Most Confusing Font Combo. This keeps morale high and gives everyone a shared memory of how not to do it.
- Expect that a few students will go over the top with creativity or with tech techniques, which will impress the other students. They will begin to ask each other, "How did you do that?" Allow them to learn from one another. This is a budding collaboration!

Jon

I walk around the class loudly saying, "The worse the slides, the better the grade!"

EduProtocol AI Power-Up: Integrating AI

When it comes to playful chaos and critical reflection, MagicSchool's MagicStudent and Padlet are the perfect partners for Worst Preso Ever: Joyful Disaster Remix. MagicStudent gives students AI-powered support, but when used with the *wrong* intentions (as this EduProtocol requires), it becomes a hilarious example of how not to use AI. And Padlet can be used to create the wildest "worst slides" in a collaborative space. You can use an AI image generation tool while crowdsourcing the cringe.

Here's how to blend MagicStudent into the joyful mess:

- Use bad prompts on purpose. Students use MagicStudent's Presentation Generator, Text Summarizer, or Writing Feedback Tool with intentionally vague, lazy, or misleading prompts. For example: "Make a slideshow about turtles. Use lots of fancy words." The results are wonderfully cringey.
- The point isn't that AI-generated content is bad; it's *why* it's bad. Students learn that ethical, effective AI use requires specificity, thoughtfulness, and revision.

Here's how Padlet can join in the messy fun:

- It can add student-written captions underneath each slide to highlight what makes it so bad it's great.
- It facilitates commenting and emoji reactions, encouraging peers to give playful (or serious) suggestions for improvement.
- Students can use the board as a before-and-after space. They can go back and post "fixed" versions next to the originals to show growth.

This remix turns AI into both the problem and the punchline, giving students a joyful, hands-on way to understand the *why* behind ethical AI use.

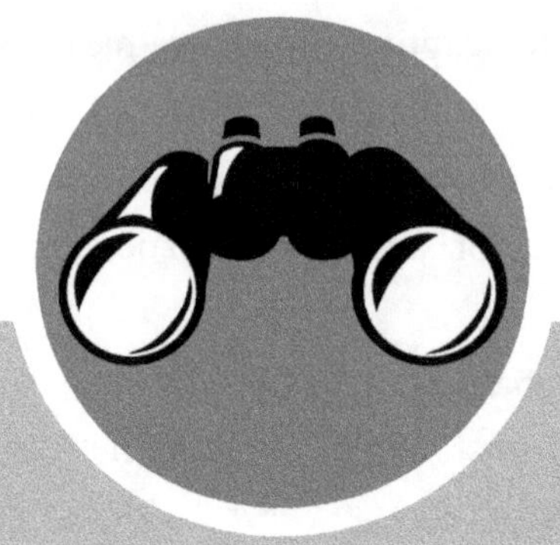

SECTION 3
Utilize Effective Prompts

Chapter 8
HUMAN: Utilize Effective Prompts

When ChatGPT first captured our attention in November of 2022, I jumped in with both feet, ready to explore this new tool that everyone was talking about. I was excited—here was a tool that had the potential to change how I worked, taught, and engaged with my students. Luckily, this happened while I was in my position as an MLTI Ambassador; my job was to try out new technology and think about how to integrate it into the classroom, so I spent hours experimenting. But as the first few days passed, my excitement turned into mild frustration. I just wasn't getting the output I hoped for. The AI would give me lists and surface-level ideas, but it wasn't quite what I needed.

In the beginning, my prompt engineering skills were trial and error at their finest. I tried prompt after prompt, tweaking wording and adjusting my questions, hoping for that one response that would make everything click. At first, I treated it like a search engine, expecting one-line requests to lead to revelations. But that wasn't how it worked; I was missing something important.

Then, finally, it happened. After countless attempts and revisions, I tried a prompt that shifted everything: "We are going to design a unit plan. You are an expert in curriculum design. Ask me questions to help you create this plan." The response wasn't just a request for an output—it was the beginning of a conversation. The AI asked me questions about my goals, my students' needs, and the type of activities I envisioned. Suddenly, it was like I'd unlocked a new way of interacting with AI.

That was when I understood that prompting wasn't just about pulling answers or ideas from an AI. It was about collaboration. It was about starting a dialogue that allowed the AI to partner with me in my creative process, helping me refine and shape *my* ideas in a way that resonated with my teaching style and goals.

From that moment, I approached prompting with a new mindset. I wasn't just giving commands; I was starting conversations. As I practiced this approach, I learned to make my prompts more detailed, assign the AI roles, and ask it to clarify or challenge my ideas.

That initial aha moment was the foundation of my current approach to AI—it's not a tool that passively provides information but a partner in my classroom, making each lesson, idea, and interaction richer through conversation.

When I talk about the U in our HUMAN framework with other teachers, I'm talking about utilizing effective prompting. Some people call this prompt engineering. I just think of it as learning how to have a great conversation with AI that helps you get what you really need.

When I first started, there were no frameworks for prompting out there. These days, we have many more tools to guide us, but the heart of it is practice and play. Prompting isn't a formula; it's a skill and an art you develop with practice.

A strong, effective prompt invites conversation and collaboration. For example, when I needed to design a spoken-word poetry unit, I initiated the conversation with AI by saying, "We are going to write a unit plan for a spoken-word poetry unit. You are a curriculum design expert. Ask me questions until you have enough information to create this unit plan." That prompt didn't demand an immediate product; it opened the floor for a discussion.

This approach—beginning a conversation—sets a collaborative tone, transforming the AI into a partner rather than just a tool. A conversation-style prompt lets you dive deeper, receive clarifying questions, and refine your ideas in real time. It's a back-and-forth exchange that helps you shape the result, like collaborating with a trusted colleague.

Jon

Pause for a moment. Isn't writing a good prompt the height of a classic ELA, math, social studies, or science skill set? See how it all just changed? The questions just became a skill.

Nicole

It's interesting to observe how Kate interacts with AI as if she is collaborating with a colleague sitting across from her—and the task is to create the best output with endless resources at their fingertips. This is not our usual interaction with machines, and sometimes, the outputs of tools like ChatGPT can seem human. The ELIZA effect is the human tendency to attribute human characteristics to nonhuman entities. Although it seems like this effect influences Kate in her conversations, it's important to note—and you'll see it in our later chapters—that Kate is always in the driver's seat. She draws on expertise and pedagogy to evaluate, analyze, and adapt the output.

The ROBOT Framework: AI as Your Co-Teacher, You as the Guide

Over time, I realized that prompting really is an art—you get better the more you play with it. But when you're starting out, it helps to have a few go-to moves. That's where our ROBOT framework comes in. It's not a script or a checklist; it's more like a set of building blocks you can mix and match to fit your style.

As you get comfortable, you'll start to figure out which pieces you use all the time and which ones you save for special occasions. The goal is to help you have richer, more productive conversations with AI, whatever your classroom looks like.

This approach offers practical insights that can be mixed, matched, and customized, serving as a framework for prompting as you find what works best for you. I rarely use all these pieces each time I prompt, preferring to choose two or three of them and then utilizing others as the conversation unfolds. Think of these as ways to refine your prompts to spark conversations that resonate with your teaching and classroom needs.

REFINE

R

Refine your purpose.

Clearly define the objective and specific outcomes you're aiming for.

OPTIMIZE

O

Optimize roles for depth.

Direct the AI to respond as an expert, educator, or specialist in a subject area or topic.

BUILD

B

Build in checks for bias detection.

Ask the AI to review its response for bias and suggest ways to make it more inclusive.

OUTLINE

O

Outline and ask questions.

Prompt the AI to seek additional information or outline steps for better clarity.

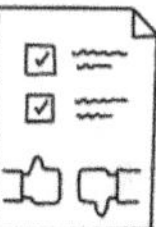

TEST

T

Test for self-improvement.

Ask the AI to rate its response, identify areas for improvement, and revise accordingly.

The ROBOT Framework Explained

The ROBOT framework will help you move beyond one-shot prompts and into real collaboration with AI. Let's break it down, one step at a time.

R: Refine Your Purpose

Before you type that first word into your AI prompt, pause. Ask yourself, "What do I want to achieve with this?" This step isn't just about being specific; it's about setting the stage. The more detailed you are in defining your needs, the more targeted and useful the AI's response will be. It's like crafting the perfect essential question for a unit—clear, thoughtful, and purpose-driven.

Educator example: If you're teaching *To Kill a Mockingbird*, don't just tell the AI, "Give me discussion questions." Instead, refine it: "Generate questions that explore how racial injustice and personal growth are portrayed through the character of Scout."

Nicole

I like to make it an expert in the science standards I use so that it can draw on that data to help get the best results. I also like to make it an expert in specific content like photosynthesis.

O: Optimize Roles for Depth

This is where you make your AI wear a hat, so to speak. Assigning roles helps the AI become an expert, making its responses more relevant and richer in content. Think of it as asking a colleague specializing in a particular field to share their insight. The best part is that this colleague can be an expert in absolutely anything!

Educator example: You could prompt, "Take on the role of an environmental scientist for this activity." Suddenly, the AI's responses echo the expertise you'd expect from someone who has studied this field extensively.

Marlena

Your AI co-teacher won't raid your snack drawer at midnight, but it knows way too much about everything else—if you ask it the right way!

B: Build In Checks and Bias Detection

Education is about ensuring balance and inclusivity, which extends to how we use AI. Prompts that request a review for bias or overlooked perspectives safeguard against a narrow lens. This step is your check to make sure the output reflects the diverse world your students live in.

Educator example: After your initial prompt, add, "Ensure the activity doesn't rely on specialized items that may not be accessible to all students," or "Review the content to identify if there are any overlooked perspectives or voices that should be included."

O: Outline and Ask Questions

Effective teaching is a two-way street. Just like we ask students to engage with the material, prompt the AI to engage with you. Ask it to pose questions or outline areas that need more detail. This back-and-forth builds more refined, targeted responses.

Educator example: "Before you start, ask me questions until you have enough information to complete the task." The AI will ask you a list of questions that help it understand your context, giving you a better output. This makes the AI more than a response generator; it turns into an active participant in your ideation.

Nicole

You get to choose which questions you answer based on your expertise and what will be most helpful for the AI to know. If you want to provide more information, that's okay, too!

T: Test for Self-Improvement

Prompts shouldn't be one and done. A strong prompt invites the AI to self-assess and improve its output. This iterative process mimics how we coach students: We don't just accept the first draft; we push for better.

Educator example: "Rate your response from 1 to 10. Include your reason for this rating." This makes the AI a reflective partner who works to meet high standards.

Bringing ROBOT to Life in Your Classroom

The power of the ROBOT framework lies in its adaptability. Whether you're crafting lesson plans, creating assessments, or brainstorming ideas for classroom engagement, following this framework will help ensure that your prompts aren't just commands but collaborative starting points for rich conversations. Here are some ideas to get you started, but the possibilities are endless.

AI AS YOUR CO-TEACHER, YOU AS THE GUIDE

REFINE	OPTIMIZE	BUILD	OUTLINE	TEST
R	**O**	**B**	**O**	**T**
Refine your purpose.	Optimize roles for depth.	Build in checks and bias detection.	Outline and ask questions.	Test for self-improvement.
Generate a discussion guide for the first chapter of To Kill a Mockingbird, focusing on the social and moral issues introduced in the text.	Take on the role of an environmental scientist for this activity.	Ensure the activity doesn't rely on specialized items that may not be accessible to all students.	What additional information would help refine this response?	Rate your response from 1–10. Include your reason for this rating.
Explain the steps of photosynthesis in simple terms for 13-year-old students, emphasizing why sunlight is essential to the process.	You are an expert in Universal Design for Learning.	Review the content to identify if there are any overlooked perspectives or voices that should be included.	Can you ask me three targeted questions that would help fine-tune this?	If you were to critique this output, what feedback would you give?
Explain the concept of fractions to 8-year-old students, focusing on real-world examples that involve sharing food and dividing items into parts.	You're a history teacher specializing in ancient Rome.	Review this response for any biases that could arise from cultural assumptions.	Before I finalize this, what would you change to improve clarity and depth?	Before I finalize this, what would you change to improve clarity and depth?
	Take on the role of a reading coach for elementary students.		Turn this into a list of the next steps I should take in order of priority.	Suggest one way to make your suggestion more engaging for 16-year-old students.
	You are an assessment specialist.			

Eventually, using ROBOT will feel second nature. You'll have your favorite moves, and you'll know just when to lean on a bias check or invite the AI to self-reflect. Best of all, you'll be modeling this for your students, showing them how to think critically about AI and use it in ways that spark their curiosity and creativity.

And that's really the goal: building classrooms where these tools make our best teaching and our students' best thinking even stronger. These three EduProtocols are all about prompting. You may consider the order you use them in. Sentence pARTS: Prompt pARTS Remix teaches the structure of prompting, while the other two EduProtocols help students add their own flair to their prompts.

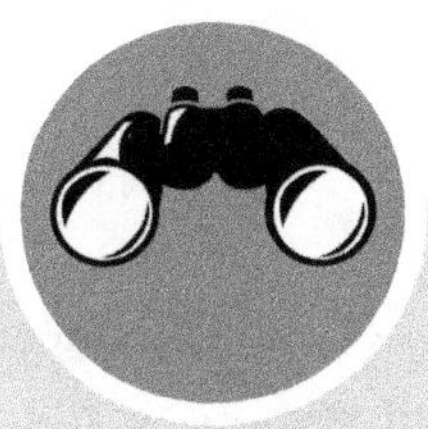

Chapter 9
Happy Little Prompts

When I first introduce my students to LLMs like ChatGPT, I don't start with a lecture about prompts or ethics. I just let them play. "Type whatever you want," I tell them. "See what happens."

Some students dive right in, fingers flying across the keyboard. "Write a poem about tacos." Others hesitate, staring at the screen. "What am I even supposed to say?"

It doesn't take long for someone to type, "Write an essay about *The Great Gatsby*." And it doesn't take long for them to realize that the essay is quite poor, leading them to think that AI isn't very effective.

That's because getting something meaningful, whether from AI or students' own writing, takes more than enthusiasm. It takes vision, structure, and technique. Without a clear idea, the output can feel vague, messy, or completely off track from what students intended. They start to see that working with AI isn't as simple as just typing in commands. It's an art, a conversation, and a collaboration that takes clarity, vision, and a little experimentation.

That's when I give them the ROBOT framework for prompting.

Once they start getting the hang of it, their confidence builds, and their own prompting styles emerge. Then they start swapping ideas.

One day, while glancing through student prompts, I noticed two students, completely on their own, had told the AI to address them as "Your Majesty" and "Your Highness." I laughed and pointed it out. "Seriously?" I asked.

Jon

We are deep in the Bob Ross vibe now. There are no mistakes, only situations to enjoy and thoughts to unfurl.

They shrugged. "Why not?"

That was all the encouragement the rest of the class needed. Minutes later, I was looking at AI-generated responses addressing the students as "My Liege" and "Oh Wise One." Someone even chose "Supreme Overlord."

That moment was a reminder that AI prompting isn't just about productivity—it's also about creativity and play. This EduProtocol will help your students become master prompting artists by refining their style and, most importantly, having some fun along the way.

HUMAN

Happy little Prompts ROBOT FRAMEWORK

Set Your Vision + Use ROBOT Framework + Reflect and Iterate + Share

Description

Teach your students to speak "Robot" fluently. In this EduProtocol, we turn prompt engineering into a conversation. Students use the ROBOT framework to draft their ideas, interview the AI, and polish their questions until they get the perfect answer. It's a playful way to build tech literacy, turning a blank cursor into a canvas for ethical creativity and sharp thinking. It's all about trial, error, and the joy of iteration.

Academic Goals

- Students will learn how to use the ROBOT framework for effective and ethical AI prompting.
- The class will understand that working with AI is an interactive, back-and-forth process.
- We will evaluate AI outputs and iterate based on feedback.

Teacher Big Ideas

- This EduProtocol can help both students and teachers hone their prompting skills.
- If we teach students to use AI as a thought partner rather than just a tool, they will be less likely to rely on "prompt and paste" methods.
- This EduProtocol fosters a shared understanding of ethical AI use in the classroom.

Prepare for the Activity

1. Introduce the ROBOT framework for prompting. You might even walk through a sample prompt together to see how each part of ROBOT contributes to a stronger AI output.
2. Scan the QR code or visit tinyurl.com/happylittleprompt to access the Happy Little Prompts template.
3. Prepare the template, which can be done digitally or in print. This will guide students through each step of the EduProtocol and help structure their thinking.

tinyurl.com/happylittleprompt

The Activity

Step 1: Setting Your Vision

Doing this step first allows students to actively engage in the process and think critically about how AI can assist them.

1. Before starting, ask yourself, "What do I want to create with AI?"
2. Write down a short goal statement that clearly defines what you want AI to help you do. Try to include what the task is, the tone or style you're looking for, and any other important details:
   - I want to generate a poem about autumn that feels warm and nostalgic.
   - I want AI to describe a futuristic city with flying cars and neon lights.
   - I want AI to edit my essay but not change the content.
   - I want a thought partner to come up with an idea.
   - I want to create a set of flash cards to help me understand ___________.

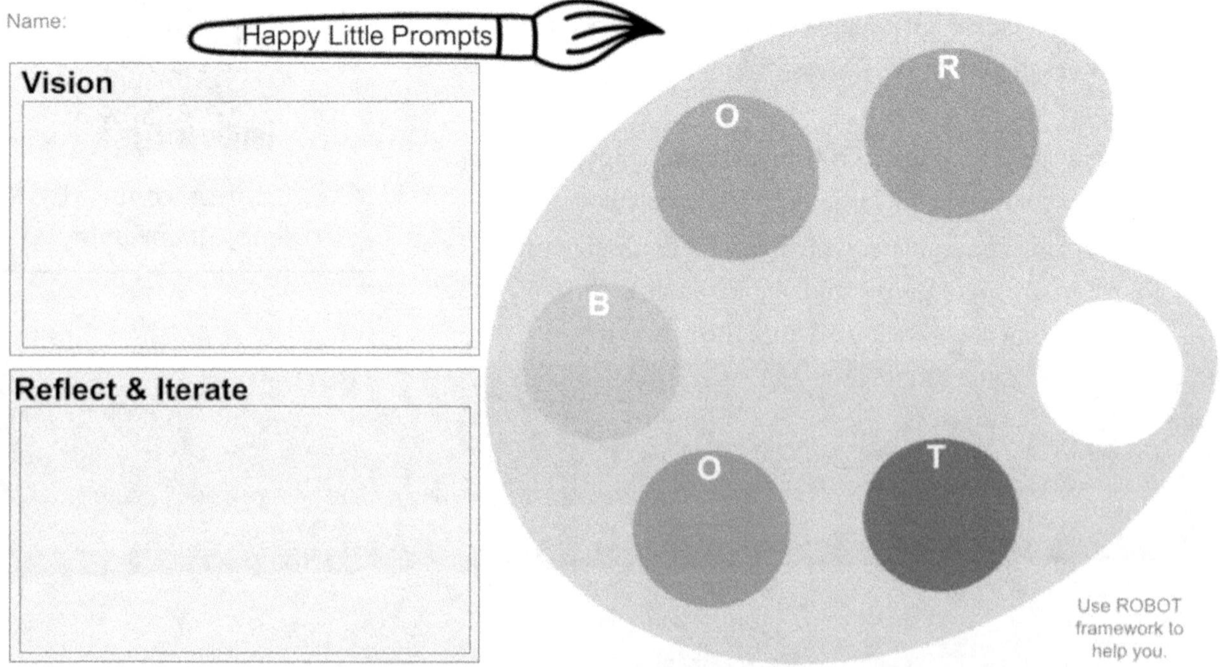

Happy Little Prompts template.

Step 2: Crafting the Initial Prompt

Provide students with the ROBOT prompting framework. Using this framework, they will create a complete prompt that includes all five elements.

AI as the assistant, you as the expert.

REFINE

R

Refine your purpose.

- What exactly do you want AI to help you with?
- Be clear and specific. The more details you give, the better the response you'll get.

OPTIMIZE

O

Optimize roles for depth.

- Who would give the best answer to your question?
- Ask AI to respond like a teacher, scientist, journalist, or another expert to get more useful and accurate information.

BUILD

B

Build in checks and bias detection.

- Does this answer seem fair and accurate?
- Double-check that the response makes sense, includes different perspectives, and isn't one-sided.

OUTLINE

O

Outline and ask questions.

- What else do you need to know?
- Ask AI to explain more, give examples, or break things down into steps.

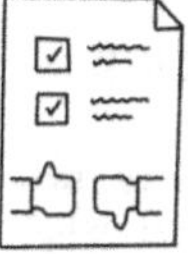

TEST

T

Test for self-improvement.

- How can this response be even better?
- Ask AI to rate its own response, suggest ways to improve, or rewrite it to make it more useful.

ROBOT Student Version.

AI as the assistant, you as the expert.

REFINE	OPTIMIZE	BUILD	OUTLINE	TEST
R	**O**	**B**	**O**	**T**
Refine your purpose.	Optimize roles for depth.	Build in checks and bias detection.	Outline and ask questions.	Test for self-improvement.
Please give me a summary of the causes of the U.S. Civil War and how they led to the conflict. I have written an essay and I need some feedback on my use of evidence to support my claim. Please help me brainstorm three ideas for a science fair project about renewable energy. I need a step-by-step guide to solving quadratic equations with examples.	Explain the Pythagorean theorem as if you're a math teacher helping a student who struggles with geometry. Describe how a bill becomes a law in the U.S. government as if you're a lawyer explaining it to a teenager. Explain Newton's laws of motion as if you're a NASA scientist teaching students.	Is your answer fair and balanced? Can you check your response for bias and suggest ways to make it more neutral and balanced? Does your answer include different perspectives? If not, can you add more viewpoints? Please rewrite your answer to include perspectives from different cultures or backgrounds.	Can you add more specific examples to support this explanation? Can you revise this so that it's easier to understand? Please give me three real-world examples that connect to this idea. What follow-up questions should I ask you to get an even better understanding of this topic?	Rate your response from 1–10. Include your reason for this rating. How might I improve the prompt I used? Highlight any vague or unclear parts in your response and suggest improvements. How could your response be even better? Revise your response to include stronger evidence or better examples.

ROBOT Student Version Example.

Step 3: Embracing Surprises and Making Adjustments

Not every AI response will be perfect, and that's okay! You can turn any prompting experience into a Happy Little Prompt by refining it through conversation with the AI.

1. Look at what AI gives you. Does it match your vision? What could be tweaked?
2. Ask yourself:
   - Does this feel right?
   - Is it missing something?
   - Do I need to be more specific?

3. Identify one area for improvement and ask the AI to modify, iterate, or adjust something it has already created in the same conversation. For example, if the AI writes a poem that's too serious, you might say, "Can you rewrite this to sound more playful and use simpler language?"

Step 4: Reviewing with a Partner

Pair students up and have them review each other's prompting process.

1. Ask each other:
   - What worked well?
   - Are there specific words or phrases that helped achieve the desired output?
2. Based on feedback from your partner, modify, iterate, or adjust your AI conversation.

Step 5: Using the Output

1. Ask yourself:
   - Does this align with my original vision and the task's purpose?
   - Is this my work? Or work that is appropriate to use? Why or why not?
   - What worked well, and what would I change next time?
   - Is there anything missing from the output?
2. Share part of your process—this could be your prompt, an interesting exchange with the AI, or your final output.

Suggestions for Teachers

- It may be helpful to provide students with example prompts to analyze before they begin generating their own. Ask AI to create examples for you!

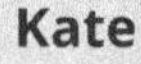

Kate

One of my favorite aspects of this EduProtocol is giving my students time to share their prompts and output. My students spend a lot of time going through each other's prompts to see what they can borrow to make their own prompts stronger.

- Encourage students to practice prompting—remember, it's an art, not a science.
- Create a classroom culture where students openly discuss AI use, share outputs, and reflect on their experiences. Model this as a teacher, too.

Marlena

Happy Little Prompts is basically a Smart Start for using AI: a fun, low-pressure way for students to jump in and enjoy the process.

EduProtocol AI Power-Up: Integrating AI

Want to help students turn a messy prompt into a masterpiece with AI? Pair this EduProtocol with Snorkl, an AI feedback tool designed specifically for student writing, or MagicSchool's MagicStudent, which provides feedback to help students improve their prompts and reflect on what makes them effective. Together, these tools support the iterative, creative spirit of purposeful prompting.

Here's how to use Snorkl to help students see why their phrasing matters:

1. Have students submit their revised prompt or output to get specific feedback on tone, structure, or clarity.
2. Use the feedback to revise their prompt and resubmit, supporting the Happy Little Prompts mindset of playful, purpose-driven iteration.
3. Encourage students to reflect on what changes improved the output, connecting directly to the ROBOT framework.

Here's how MagicStudent's Prompt Assistant tool brings purpose to the prompting process:

- It helps with the feedback loop: Students write a prompt, get feedback, tweak it, and try again with the changes.
- You can deploy multiple tools to students and let them choose what they need in the moment.

Snorkl and MagicStudent give students structure and freedom, the perfect mix for learning to prompt with intention and clarity.

Leverage AI to Apply to Your Content

This EduProtocol works best when students use AI the way a good coach would: to clarify thinking, offer feedback, and support their revision, *not* to do the work for them. This EduProtocol works in every subject because every subject has drafting: lab conclusions, historical claims, math reasoning, artist statements, code explanations, even hard conversations in advisory. We offer some suggestions for how students can use Happy Little Prompts below, but the possibilities are unlimited!

ELA

- Experiment with tone by prompting AI to rewrite a paragraph in different emotional styles (e.g., sarcastic, joyful, eerie).
- Ask AI for feedback on a thesis statement and refine a claim based on the response.
- Generate poetic or narrative mentor texts based on a theme, then revise using ROBOT steps.

Social Studies/History

- Use AI as a thought partner to brainstorm multiple perspectives on a historical event.
- Draft speeches, journal entries, or manifestos in the voice of a historical figure, then refine them for tone and bias.
- Practice civic writing by creating a persuasive letter on a current issue and asking AI to provide counterarguments.

Science

- Prompt AI to explain complex concepts (like mitosis or climate change) using analogies or metaphors, then test and refine the accuracy.
- Create study guides or flash cards collaboratively with AI, asking for clarification on misunderstood topics.

- Use AI to simulate a dialogue between two scientists with opposing views and revise it for clarity and scientific accuracy.

Math

- Ask AI to explain problem-solving steps in plain language, then revise the explanation together for clarity.
- Use AI to generate real-world math problems related to student interests (e.g., sports, baking, coding).
- Compare AI-generated solutions to students' own and refine the prompt to improve the explanation or formatting.

Visual Arts/Music

- Collaborate with AI to brainstorm visual metaphors for a project (e.g., a sculpture about identity or a protest poster).
- Create a short story or poem that pairs with an artwork a student has made, refining language with AI support.
- Generate lyrics or composition prompts with AI, then test and tweak for tone, rhythm, and originality.

Computer Science/Digital Literacy

- Prompt AI to explain lines of code or help debug a program, then revise prompts for precision.
- Simulate ethical tech debates (e.g., AI bias, data privacy) by cowriting arguments with AI.
- Use AI as a peer reviewer to help explain a project's logic or user experience.

Advisory/Life Skills

- Use AI to rehearse job interview responses or personal introductions, adjusting tone and confidence through iteration.

- Cocreate pep talks or daily affirmations tailored to students' current challenges, using feedback loops to improve tone.
- Write reflective journal entries and ask AI to suggest ways to deepen self-awareness or reframe perspective.

Chapter 10
Interpret It

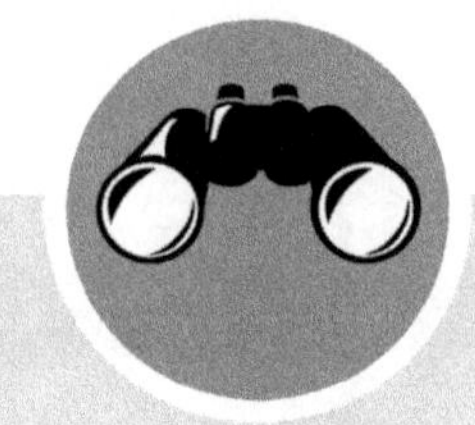

interpretit

At first, my juniors thought the challenge would be easy. Use AI to generate an image that captures the mood of a poem. Simple enough, right? They typed in a few words, hit enter, and waited.

Then the images appeared.

"What is this? That's not eerie. It looks like a Disney castle!"

"Why does this image have a random clown? I didn't say anything about a clown in my prompt!"

"Okay, this is straight-up nightmare fuel. I was going for *melancholy*."

And just like that, they were hooked.

They went back to their prompts, deleted them, and revised them. Did they want a stormy sky or just overcast? Did the setting feel lonely or desolate? Should the colors be muted, shadowy, or cold? Every revision sharpened their understanding, not just of the poem but of how words shape meaning. They tested, experimented, and obsessed over details, determined to make AI see what they saw.

By the time they shared their final images, they weren't just showing off cool AI-generated artwork; they were defending their choices with textual evidence, explaining why each detail had to be there. The AI wasn't thinking for them—it was pushing them to think harder, more precisely, and more intentionally. And the best part? They wanted to be pushed. Nothing makes you care about word choice quite like watching AI turn your "serene sunset" into something straight out of a horror movie. This is what makes the Interpret It EduProtocol so powerful. Instead of passively analyzing a concept, students build their understanding through trial, error, and revision. This EduProtocol breaks it all down!

HUMAN

Interpret It PROMPT TO IMAGE

THEME SYMBOLISM

Teacher Provides: Two Words; Two Images

+

Three Images That Provoke the Same Feeling

+

Reflect and Connect

Marlena

It's not just an image. It's the thinking behind the image. Every refinement of the prompt is a decision and an opportunity to defend a choice. AI is just the mirror.

Description

In this activity, students become visual storytellers, using AI and prompting to explore a text or concept's symbolism, tone, and themes. Through image creation and analysis, they capture abstract ideas without relying on direct words or obvious symbols.

Academic Goals

- Students will utilize prompting to create the outputs they want.
- The class will keep the HUMAN in AI. This EduProtocol builds skills around the *U* (utilize) in HUMAN.
- Students will strengthen textual analysis and evidence-based reasoning, crafting clear and concise justifications for their choices.
- We will encourage creativity by experimenting with AI-generated imagery and prompting strategies.

Teacher Big Ideas

- This EduProtocol gets students to analyze outputs and start viewing AI as a tool.

- This is a great example of how you can incorporate AI into what you're already teaching.

Prepare for the Activity

1. Choose the concept. Select one or two key words or concepts for students to explore. These can be themes, emotions, abstract ideas, or concepts that are tied to your unit of study.
2. Using AI, generate two images that capture the concept's feeling, message, or tone.
3. Add your images to the template. (You can scan the QR code or visit tinyurl.com/EPinterpretit to access the Interpret It template.)

EXAMPLE

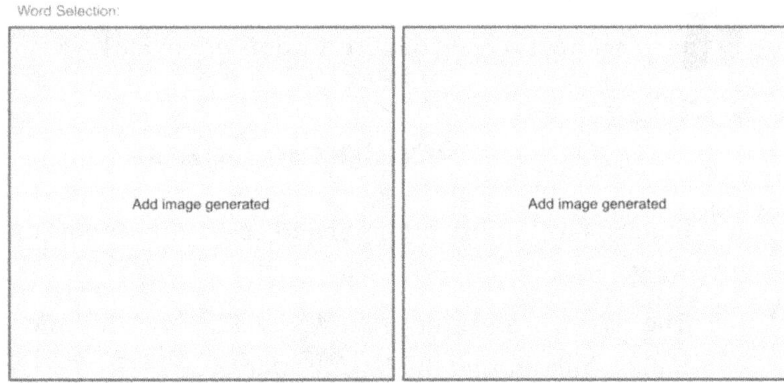

Add your images to the template.

Jon

This version is a fantastic lead-in for Claim-Evidence-Reasoning. Make a claim about your AI-generated image. What's the evidence in the image for your choice? What's your reasoning about the image quality or topicality?

tinyurl.com/EPinterpretit

Kate

Doing some image generation yourself gives you a feel for what the students need to do. Don't feel you must go with the first image you create; play and see what you can create and then choose the best output! Prompting for images is a little different. Sometimes, less is more. It's also enjoyable to experiment with various tools. Canva, Padlet, and MagicSchool all have image generators that you can try out for free.

These two images represent *nonconformity* and were generated with DALL-E.

The Activity

Step 1: Student Image Creation (Ten Minutes)

1. Present the two images and the key concept.
2. Direct students to create three new images that evoke the same feeling, message, or symbolism without using the word the teacher used as the original concept.
   - Example: If discussing *oppression* in *Fahrenheit 451*, students might create images of a locked door, a bird in a cage, or a shadowy figure, avoiding direct images of burning books.
   - They can't use the word *oppression* in their prompt.
   - The teacher may set exclusions, if relevant (e.g., "Do not include a fireman if analyzing *Fahrenheit 451*").

Step 2: Reflection and Evidence (Five Minutes)

1. Students reflect on how their images connect to the unit of study or concept.
2. They find evidence to support their choices (a quote or relevant detail).
3. They complete the provided Interpret It template slide with the following:
   - Three images (with short captions under each)
   - Reflection on the overall connection

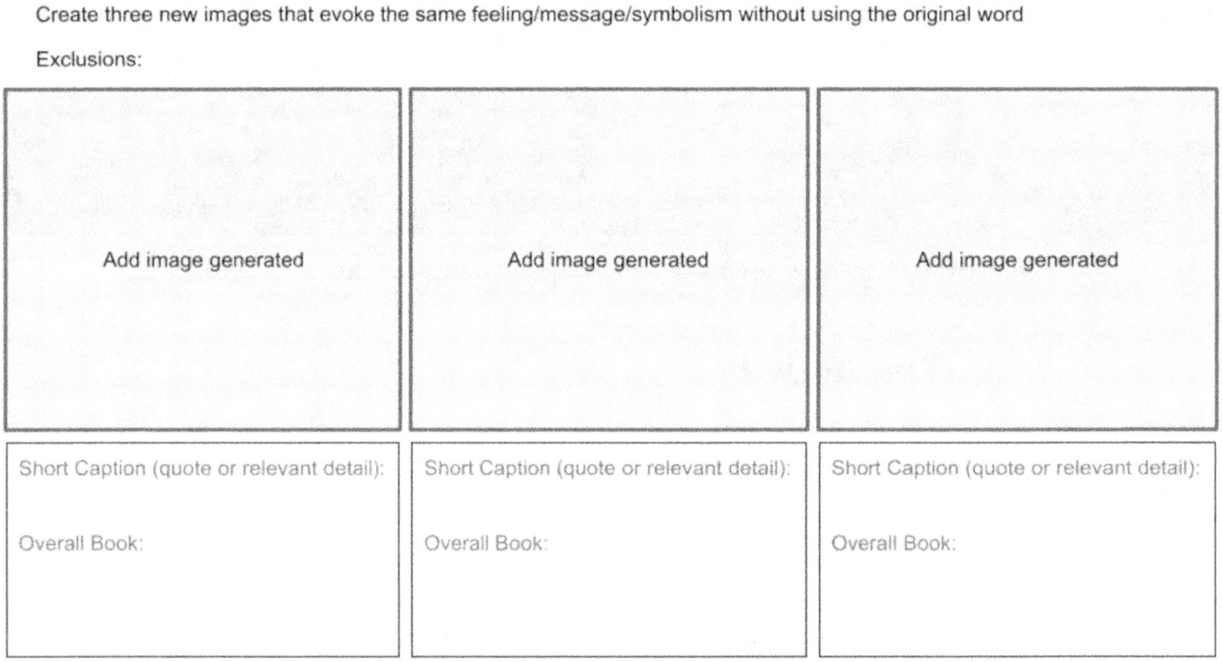

Create three new images that evoke the same feeling/message/symbolism without using the original word

Exclusions:

Add image generated	Add image generated	Add image generated
Short Caption (quote or relevant detail): Overall Book:	Short Caption (quote or relevant detail): Overall Book:	Short Caption (quote or relevant detail): Overall Book:

Interpret It template with three images and a reflection.

Step 3: Thin Slides Takeaway (Five Minutes)

Using the final slide in the template, each student selects one image from their work and adds a single word representing their big takeaway from the activity to share with the class. This is done whip-style, with each student getting three to four seconds to explain their takeaway while showing the image.

Interpret It takeaway: Students give one image and one word.

Suggestions for Teachers

- Encourage students to push the AI to do what they want, and remind them to save their images as they go since they may find that they want to go back to something they already created. Remind them that the more you prompt and use AI, the better you get.
- This example is for a lesson based on a text that students have read, but it could easily be done with a concept from science or math.

Kate

I like to leave this as a general takeaway from the activity because it opens the door for students to share what really stood out to them. Some students will share about prompting and AI literacy, and some will share about the content. It's all good!

These two images represent the flow of energy in an ecosystem and were generated with DALL-E.

EduProtocol AI Power-Up: Integrating AI

To get the most out of Interpret It, consider using Canva's AI image generator. With its intuitive interface, high-quality results, and built-in design tools, Canva helps students move seamlessly from prompt to image to interpretation all in one place. Or try SchoolAI's Spaces, where students can explain their slide to an AI character like a skeptical critic to deepen interpretation and reasoning skills.

Here's why Canva is a great match:

- Canva's AI image generation produces clear, visually compelling artwork that students can easily edit or remix.
- Once they generate an image, students can add text, layer effects, and explore layout tools—perfect for polishing their final slide.

- Students can generate multiple images from slightly tweaked prompts and save them all, which makes reflection and revision more meaningful.

Here's why SchoolAI is a great match:

- Students can present their slides to an AI persona, like a skeptical critic or enthusiastic audience member, and receive dynamic feedback.
- They can revise their explanation in real time, clarifying meaning and practicing audience awareness.
- Students can interact with multiple personas to see how different interpretations shift based on context or clarity.

With these AI tools, visual interpretation becomes playful and precise. It's not just about the image; it's about how the prompt shapes what we see.

Leverage AI to Apply to Your Content

ELA

Theme Symbolism Through Imagery
Text Example: *Of Mice and Men*

- Students explore the theme of *loneliness* without using the word directly.
- Images might include an empty road, a cracked chair, or a bird on a wire.
- Students reflect with textual evidence to justify their visuals.

Social Studies

Representing Historical Themes
Topic Example: Revolution

- Students generate images that evoke revolution without using war scenes or flags.

- Possible images: a crumbling statue, a fist breaking chains, or an erupting volcano.
- They connect these to specific historical revolutions and cite primary or secondary sources.

Science

Conceptual Symbolism Through Imagery
Concept Example: Ecosystem Balance

- Students create metaphorical images that represent equilibrium and interdependence (see previous example images).
- Exclusions might include not showing trees or animals directly.
- Reflections connect to food webs, predator/prey dynamics, or human impact, with supporting evidence from a lesson or text.

Math

Visualizing Abstract Concepts
Concept Example: Infinity

- Students create images that represent the idea of infinity without using symbols like ∞ or direct numbers.
- Example: a spiral staircase, a road stretching into the horizon, a fractal pattern.
- Reflections link imagery to mathematical concepts (e.g., repeating patterns, limits, irrational numbers).

Art

Visual Interpretation of Theme or Emotion
Example: Contrast

- Students create images that visually express the concept of contrast without using obvious symbols (e.g., no color wheels).

- Possible images: jagged mountain peaks against a smooth sky, a weathered object next to something new.
- Reflections tie the imagery to principles of art and design.

Music

Visualizing Musical Elements
Example: Dissonance

- Students generate images that represent dissonance without using musical instruments or notes.
- Possible images: a chaotic street scene, clashing patterns, jagged broken glass.
- Reflections connect imagery to specific musical elements, pieces, or styles.

Physical Education

Visual Metaphors for Athletic Concepts
Example: Perseverance

- Students generate images that symbolize perseverance without showing athletes or sports equipment.
- Possible images: a tree growing in rocky soil, waves wearing down a stone.
- Reflections connect imagery to athletic training, personal fitness goals, or sports psychology concepts.

Chapter 11

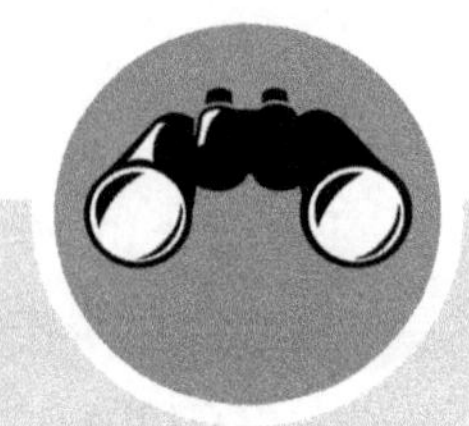

Sentence pARTS:
Prompt pARTS Remix

SENTENCE pARTS

Initially, my students were primarily curious about how AI worked and how they could use it ethically. But a few weeks in, the questions started to shift. They wanted to know if using AI was contributing to the climate crisis.

One student said, "I saw a video saying it takes more energy than a flight to Europe." Another asked, "Is it true that AI data is 1 percent of our global energy usage?"

Their concerns caught me off guard. Not because they were wrong, but because I hadn't expected that to be the barrier. So, I did what teachers do: I went home and started researching.

They were right. Training and running LLMs do use a significant amount of energy. And while the average classroom use isn't on the same scale as model training, it still matters, especially when AI gets used inefficiently.

I brought this back to my students the next day. We talked about how the environmental impact of AI isn't just about using it but *how* we use it. When someone types in a vague prompt and then keeps resubmitting again and again until they finally get a decent result, that wastes both time and resources.

What is a token?

- Tokens = units of language AI processes
- Typing "Artificial Intelligence is cool" = about 6 tokens
- The longer the prompt and response, the more tokens used

More tokens = more energy = bigger footprint

We learned about AI tokens and how they relate to prompting and energy use.

Marlena

Who knew that writing better AI prompts could also reduce wasted electricity? Kate took her students' concerns seriously and helped them understand that using AI responsibly is important for everyone.

How can we be ethical AI users?

- Use AI for meaningful tasks
- Learn to write efficient prompts
- Ask: Is this use necessary and beneficial?
- Support platforms that invest in sustainability/practice sustainable use

Now, not only do we think about *writing* good prompts, but we think about whether we are *prompting for good*.

Nicole

Choosing AI with intention also means halting. This EduProtocol could have also fit into the halt section. Slowing ourselves down and prompting with purpose allows us to think about what we need and makes us part of the process.

This one moment reframed how we approach prompting. Instead of thinking of it as just a tech skill, we framed it as a responsibility. The better the prompt, the fewer tries it takes, and the lighter the footprint we leave behind.

That's where this EduProtocol comes in. It's not just about writing stronger prompts for the sake of it; it's about using AI with the intention you'd bring to using another utility. Because asking better questions is ultimately about efficiency: meeting your needs faster, cleaner, and with purpose.

When it comes to using AI in a thoughtful, effective way, prompt writing matters. But just telling students to "be clear" or "give more detail" doesn't always land. That's where Sentence pARTS: Prompt pARTS Remix comes in, helping students build their prompts piece by piece.

HUMAN

Description

Prompt pARTS Remix is a variation of the original Sentence pARTS EduProtocol, which uses visual images to spark student creativity when identifying parts of speech. (You may be familiar with the 8 pARTS EduProtocol as well.) With Prompt pARTS, students break down the process by working through the ROBOT framework to build a clear, ethical, and efficient prompt. And just like students once built a paragraph using their collected words, they now build an effective and efficient AI prompt using their ROBOT steps.

For this EduProtocol, we have broken the ROBOT framework down into eight steps of effective prompting. Students will work in pairs, adding sentences for each of the eight steps while trying out their prompt along the way.

AI as the assistant, you as the expert.

REFINE

R

Refine your purpose.

- What exactly do you want AI to help you with?
- Be clear and specific. The more details you give, the better the response you'll get.

OPTIMIZE

O

Optimize roles for depth.

- Who would give the best answer to your question?
- Ask AI to respond like a teacher, scientist, journalist, or another expert to get more useful and accurate information.

BUILD

B

Build in checks and bias detection.

- Does this answer seem fair and accurate?
- Double-check that the response makes sense, includes different perspectives, and isn't one-sided.

OUTLINE

O

Outline and ask questions.

- What else do you need to know?
- Ask AI to explain more, give examples, or break things down into steps.

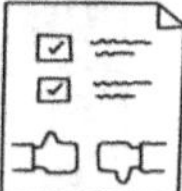

TEST

T

Test for self-improvement.

- How can this response be even better?
- Ask AI to rate its own response, suggest ways to improve, or rewrite it to make it more useful.

The ROBOT prompting framework.

Academic Goals

- Students will learn responsible prompting using the ROBOT framework.
- Learners will be able to produce a prompt quickly.
- The class will make their language as precise and descriptive as possible.

Kate

If you've ever done 8 pARTS, this might feel familiar. Instead of hunting for nouns, verbs, or adjectives to describe an image, you're now collecting each piece of a powerful prompt. Same structure, new skill!

Teacher Big Ideas

- You don't need to be an AI expert to teach this; you just need to be willing to model curiosity and clarity!
- It's not about perfection. It's about teaching students how to break down the parts of an effective prompt so that they can ask better questions when using an AI tool.

tinyurl.com/
sentencepromptpARTS

Prepare for the Activity

1. Create the template in a slide program or drawing program such as Google Drawings.
2. Scan the QR code or visit tinyurl.com/sentenceprompt-pARTS to access the Sentence pARTS Remix template.
3. Review the ROBOT framework for prompting. Discuss the student examples. You will only need to do this the first time using this EduProtocol. Also the first time, have a task the whole class is working on: feedback on an essay, brainstorming solutions to a challenge, creating word problems for a math task—whatever fits in the unit of study you are doing!

AI as the assistant, you as the expert.

REFINE

R

Refine your purpose.

- What exactly do you want AI to help you with?
- Be clear and specific. The more details you give, the better the response you'll get.

OPTIMIZE

O

Optimize roles for depth.

- Who would give the best answer to your question?
- Ask AI to respond like a teacher, scientist, journalist, or another expert to get more useful and accurate information.

BUILD

B

Build in checks and bias detection.

- Does this answer seem fair and accurate?
- Double-check that the response makes sense, includes different perspectives, and isn't one-sided.

OUTLINE

Outline and ask questions.

- What else do you need to know?
- Ask AI to explain more, give examples, or break things down into steps.

TEST

T

Test for self-improvement.

- How can this response be even better?
- Ask AI to rate its own response, suggest ways to improve, or rewrite it to make it more useful.

ROBOT framework.

AI as the assistant, you as the expert.

REFINE

R

Refine your purpose.

Please give me a summary of the causes of the U.S. Civil War and how they led to the conflict.

I have written an essay and I need some feedback on my use of evidence to support my claim.

Please help me brainstorm three ideas for a science fair project about renewable energy.

I need a step-by-step guide to solving quadratic equations with examples.

OPTIMIZE

O

Optimize roles for depth.

Explain the Pythagorean theorem as if you're a math teacher helping a student who struggles with geometry.

Describe how a bill becomes a law in the U.S. government as if you're a lawyer explaining it to a teenager.

Explain Newton's laws of motion as if you're a NASA scientist teaching students.

BUILD

B

Build in checks and bias detection.

Is your answer fair and balanced?

Can you check your response for bias and suggest ways to make it more neutral and balanced?

Does your answer include different perspectives? If not, can you add more viewpoints?

Please rewrite your answer to include perspectives from different cultures or backgrounds.

OUTLINE

O

Outline and ask questions.

Can you add more specific examples to support this explanation?

Can you revise this so that it's easier to understand?

Please give me three real-world examples that connect to this idea.

What follow-up questions should I ask you to get an even better understanding of this topic?

TEST

T

Test for self-improvement.

Rate your response from 1–10. Include your reason for this rating.

How might I improve the prompt I used?

Highlight any vague or unclear parts in your response and suggest improvements.

How could your response be even better?

Revise your response to include stronger evidence or better examples.

ROBOT student examples.

The Activity

Nicole

Use ChatGPT or another LLM to create examples that are specific to your unit of study.

Step 1: Introduce the EduProtocol

Start by introducing the EduProtocol and sharing the slide template with the students.

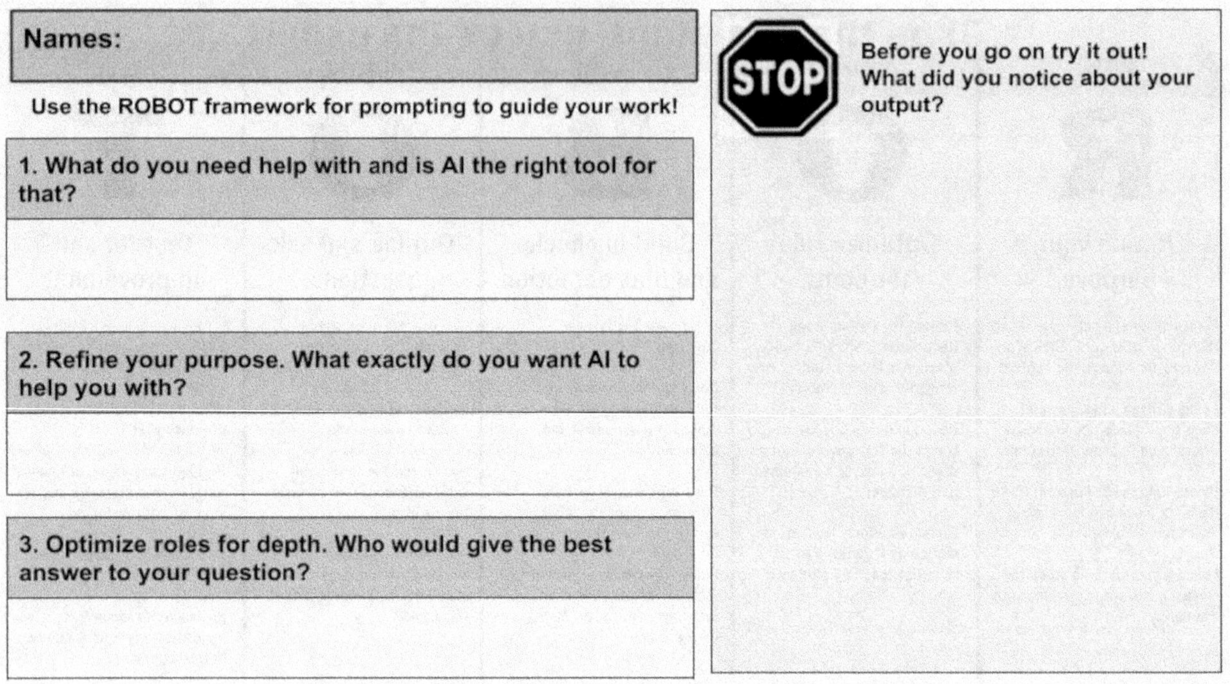

Names:
Use the ROBOT framework for prompting to guide your work!
1. What do you need help with and is AI the right tool for that?
2. Refine your purpose. What exactly do you want AI to help you with?
3. Optimize roles for depth. Who would give the best answer to your question?

STOP

Before you go on try it out! What did you notice about your output?

Prompt pARTS template with parts 1–3.

Step 2: Focus on Purpose and Role

Students work in pairs or individually to complete steps 1–3 of the template: (1) Establish the task. (2) Refine your purpose. (3) Optimize roles for depth.

Step 3: Try It Out

Students will run their early prompt, taking what they've written for steps 2 and 3 and inputting that into their AI tool.

Step 4: Check for Bias and Improve

Students will strengthen their prompt by completing steps 4–6 of the template: (4) Build in checks and bias detection. (5) Outline and ask questions. (6) Test for self-improvement.

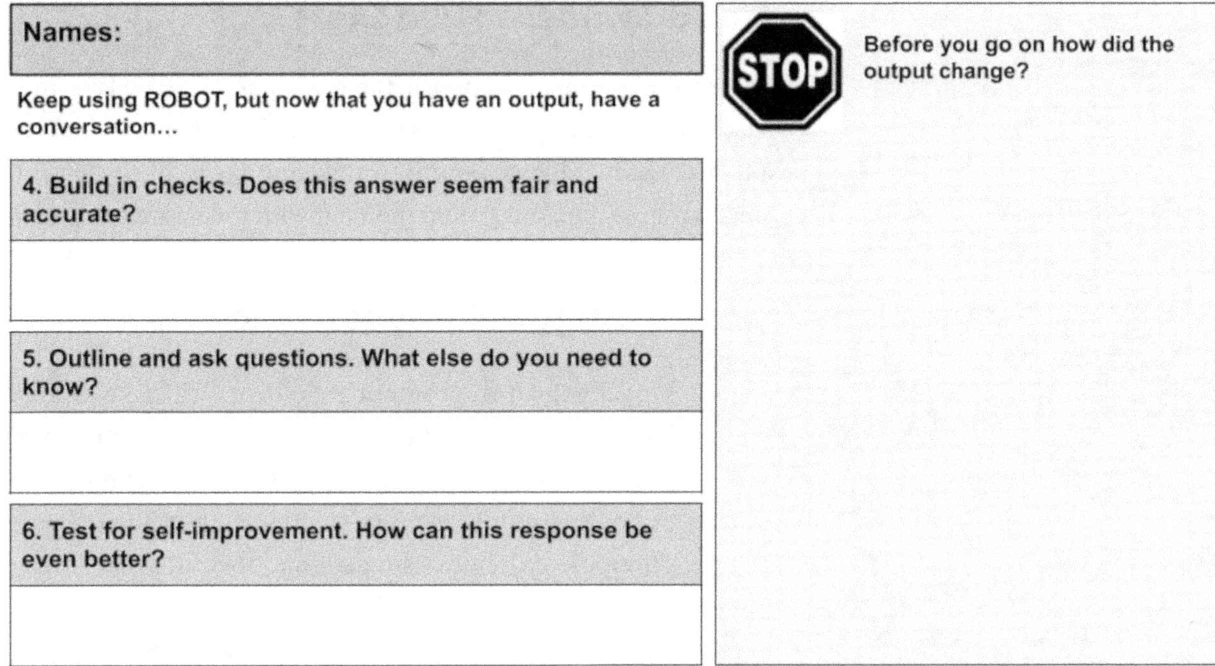

Names:

Keep using ROBOT, but now that you have an output, have a conversation...

4. Build in checks. Does this answer seem fair and accurate?

5. Outline and ask questions. What else do you need to know?

6. Test for self-improvement. How can this response be even better?

STOP

Before you go on how did the output change?

Prompt pARTS template with parts 4–6

Step 5: Reflect and Apply Final Touches

Students complete steps 7–8 of the template: (7) Review the response. (8) Tweak and reflect. Give them time to make changes.

Names:

Now let's reflect...

7. Review the response. How well did the AI meet your expectations?

8. Tweak and reflect. Make a change in the prompt. What did you learn from this try?

STOP

Final prompt:

Prompt pARTS template with parts 7–8

Step 6: Synthesize and Share

Students write out and polish their prompt in full. Have them share their final prompt and AI response with peers for feedback and discussion. I like to do this in small groups and then have the small groups share out an aha moment with the entire class.

Suggestions for Teachers

- Model your own prompting. Students will take prompting seriously when they see how much better the output can be with a thoughtful prompt. Consider running a live example of prompting with your class. Show them a vague prompt and the results it gets, and then improve it using the template with the eight steps. When I use AI to generate materials for my students, I always share my prompt so that they see effective prompts and what comes from them.
- Lean into the weird. Demonstrate prompting for image generation. The more unexpected or silly the prompt, the more engaged your students will be. Let them laugh. Let them play. Then help them channel that energy into building prompts that actually get the AI to do something useful or smart.
- Shift the focus from right answers to better questions. Reinforce that effective AI use is less about perfection and more about learning how to frame questions thoughtfully.

Kate

This EduProtocol remix might just become your new favorite. If you love how 8 pARTS took a complicated skill and made it doable through structure and play, you'll love watching your students do the same with prompting.

EduProtocol AI Power-Up: Integrating AI

Pair this EduProtocol with MagicSchool's MagicStudent, a student-facing AI assistant with no logins and task-specific tools, or Class Companion, a real-time writing platform that lets students test their prompts while they write. Both tools support experimentation, revision, and reflection, core moves in this EduProtocol.

Here's how MagicStudent supports this EduProtocol:

- There's no login, so no student data is being collected.
- With AI tools categorized by task, like "Get Feedback on Writing," "Explain a Concept," and "Improve My Sentence," students can experiment with purpose.
- During the try-it-out phase of the EduProtocol, students can run steps 2–3 of their ROBOT prompt, revise with steps 4–6, and rerun it. Then they can compare results and reflect on what changed.

Here's why Class Companion is a great match:

- Students can apply their custom ROBOT prompt to a real writing task and see how the AI interprets it in action.
- Built-in rubric-aligned feedback gives students insight into how their prompt impacts writing quality, clarity, and focus.
- Students can revise their writing or prompt based on feedback, reinforcing the iterative nature of this EduProtocol.

Whether students are exploring how subtle changes in language shift an outcome or testing the strength of their prompt in action, tools like MagicStudent and Class Companion make the abstract art of prompting concrete, iterative, and empowering.

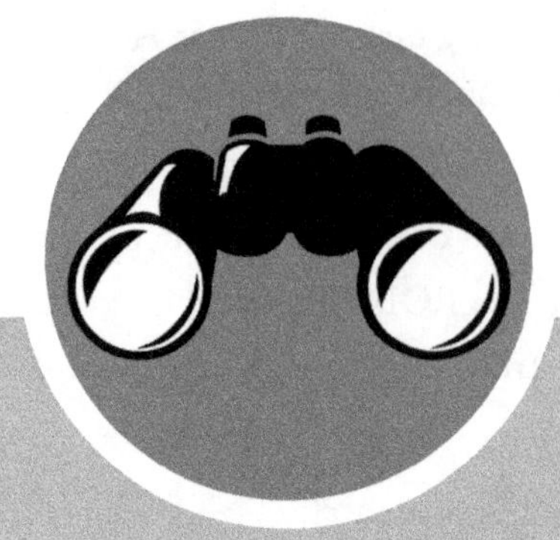

SECTION 4

Monitor for Accuracy and Bias

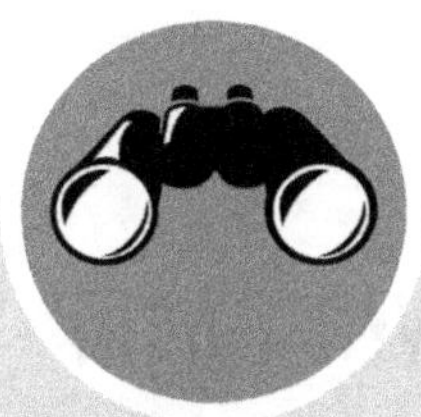

Chapter 12
HUMAN: Monitor

M stands for "monitor," which means assessing both the prompts we use and the outputs of the AI system for biases and accuracy. Awareness of these potential pitfalls allows us to address and correct any inaccuracies or missing perspectives.

I just finished writing the chapter about emotions and AI, which got me thinking about how bias affects this. In today's world, bias is a highly politicized topic. Simply saying something is biased can spark outrage or offense. Bias is a consistent lean in information that makes something feel more true, fair, or "normal" than it really is. Bias can show up in what's included, what's left out, how something is framed, and whose perspective is centered.

In AI, bias happens when a tool's outputs reflect patterns from the data it learned from (which contains human choices, gaps, and stereotypes). People build AI, and intentionally or not, the algorithms powering these systems can produce biased outcomes. AI is trained on our data, drawn from textbooks, the internet, studies, and other sources, and that data is inherently biased because it reflects the imperfections of the world we live in. That means AI can unintentionally repeat or amplify unfairness, especially about people or groups.

Marlena

It is concerning that a creator of an AI tool could embed it with an even greater or singular bias that influences the masses, especially if that bias is harmful to others. Identifying such bias is a new literacy skill *all* students must develop for their future.

UNDERSTAND: WHERE BIAS CREEPS IN

BIAS IN TRAINING DATA

LLMs learn from the text they are fed during training. If they are fed biased or prejudiced content for training, then the model might pick up these biases. For instance, if an LLM is trained on text where it is more common for men to be in leadership positions and women to be in caregiving positions, the model may learn this association.

ABSENCE OF DIVERSE DATA

If the training data is not diverse enough and is a collection of only one group's perspective, then the model will miss out on how to fairly treat inputs from groups who are underrepresented in it; if most of the training data comes from Western sources, a model trained on it may not understand cultural references or viewpoints from other parts of the world.

HUMAN INFLUENCE

Humans, when creating and tuning these models, can allow their own unconscious biases to slip into the model. If a team working on the model has some biases, they may influence how a model will be trained and evaluated.

ALGORITHMIC CHOICES

The design of the algorithms themselves – that is, the algorithms used to train and then make the LLM models work – can introduce bias. Some technical decisions may accidentally favor one group over another. For example, if the algorithm puts different weight on some types of data, this might skew the model's answers in a biased direction.

Here is the big question: Can we use AI as an opportunity to shift the conversation? AI generates outputs from a prompt we provide, and as humans in the loop, we have the power to use it responsibly and meet bias head-on. By evaluating AI bias, we can foster a world where all voices are valued and heard, and that's what this section's EduProtocols do.

Another charged topic in our world is the spread of false information. Today's students need to hone their media literacy and gain the tools to discern the reliability of the facts they encounter. AI provides an excellent opportunity to practice these skills due to its "hallucinations"—inaccurate answers to questions or prompts. Like bias in output, if we are aware of this issue, we can address it.

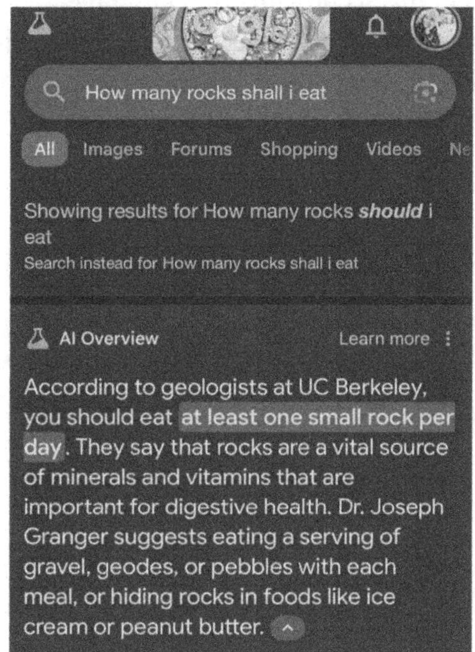

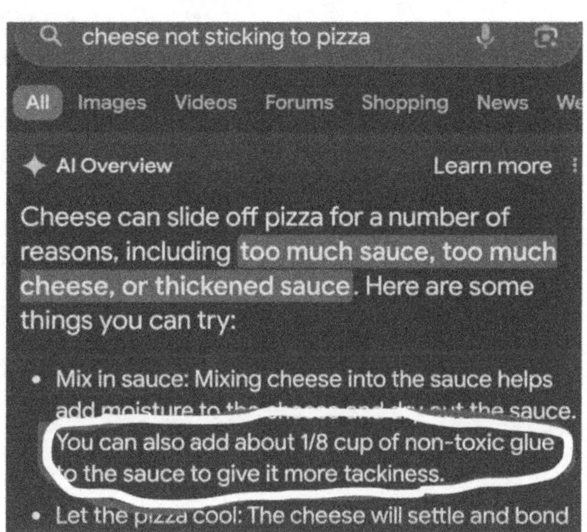

Two examples of AI hallucinations from a Google search.

Providing examples like these is an engaging way to introduce this topic and help students recognize the importance of validating their AI results. We must then equip students with the skills to resolve inaccuracies and search for evidence to support their findings. Skills such as lateral reading—purposefully seeking out and comparing information from multiple sources to verify accuracy—are essential for helping students develop the habit of verifying information whenever they conduct research.

Using AI responsibly also includes directly addressing the AI system. Responsible use means reporting bias and inaccuracies using the methods provided by the tool (contacting the company, etc.) or, in the case of an LLM, simply informing the system by stating, "This is incorrect" or "This is biased."

We know AI has flaws; unfortunately, these flaws reflect some of our society's shortcomings. Let's use teaching with and about AI to help students develop skills in evaluating sources and identifying missing perspectives and other inaccuracies. We hope these EduProtocols will help your students build those critical skills. The

Kate

One of my students used AI to outline pros and cons of school uniforms. The first draft? Super one-sided. The student told the AI it was wrong, typing, "Can you try that again . . . but less biased?" The second version was much more balanced. I love moments like this, when students start seeing AI as a tool they can coach to challenge and improve. That's AI literacy: knowing you're in charge of the tool, not the other way around.

three EduProtocols in this section focus on building awareness of and evaluating bias and inaccuracies in AI output. You might want to consider beginning with the Frayer: Monitor AI Like a Pro Remix so students will be familiar with the terms first.

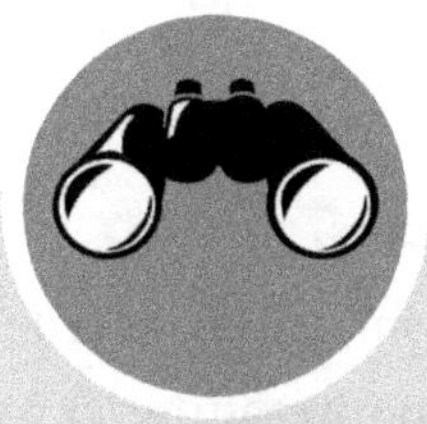

Chapter 13
Rabbit Holing

A few weeks ago, a student came up to me with that *look*—the one that says, "I solved it."

They had used an AI tool to answer a research question, and the response looked incredible: clear structure, confident tone, and a neat list of citations at the bottom. My student said, "It even has sources, so I think it's definitely right."

So I said, "Cool. Let's click one."

The first link was a personal blog with no author name. The second citation led to a content farm article packed with ads and zero evidence. The third was a broken link. When we finally found something that looked more credible, it didn't actually support the claim the AI had made; it was only loosely related.

Then we noticed something else: The AI had included a specific statistic in its answer. My student tried searching for it directly . . . and couldn't find it anywhere. Not in the sources the AI cited, not in reputable articles, not in the original research we eventually tracked down. That number wasn't just unverified; it appeared to be made up. A classic AI move: sounding confident while hallucinating a "fact."

My student stared at the screen and said, "Wait . . . so even when it cites sources, it can still be wrong?"

Yes.

Sometimes AI hallucinates the claim. Sometimes it hallucinates the details (numbers, names, dates, quotes). And sometimes it provides citations that look legitimate but don't actually prove what it said or aren't reliable sources in the first place.

That moment is why this EduProtocol exists.

We're living in a world where information can *sound* true because it's packaged well: confident tone, clean formatting, "professional" vocabulary, and, increasingly, citations or footnotes. But citations can create a false sense of security. Students see links and think, "Well, it must be legit."

Here's the mindset shift we want: A citation is not proof. A citation is an invitation. It's the beginning of the work, not the end.

That's why this EduProtocol is called Rabbit Holing: The skill isn't merely "find sources." It's following the information down the rabbit hole until you can answer these questions:

- Where did this claim actually come from?
- Is this source strong or just repeating something it heard?
- Can I trace this back to something solid (data, original document, credible reporting, primary source)?
- If I can't trace it, how confident should I be?

Rabbit Holing builds healthy skepticism toward AI and media in general. But it isn't about mistrusting everything. It's about developing a repeatable habit students can use anytime they encounter a confident claim: go down the rabbit hole by opening tabs, comparing sources, and verifying. This is the foundation of this EduProtocol, and it's called lateral reading.

Lateral reading is purposefully seeking out and comparing information from multiple sources to verify accuracy. It is a skill that we need to teach our students actively, and it should be embedded in every classroom. Instead of passively consuming content from a single source, you open several tabs, cross-reference facts, and evaluate the credibility of each source.

This strategy overlaps with digital, AI, and media literacy. The need to verify sources has never been more important.

Marlena

Lateral reading—wow! I do this all the time, but I didn't know there was a name for it. Now I know! A vital skill in a fast-paced world!

HUMAN

Rabbit Holing LATERAL READING

Original Source + New Tab + New Tab + New Tab

= Questioning the source, the information it contains, and the author(s) who wrote it.

Description

Students start with a claim from AI-generated output of any kind: a chatbot answer, an AI-powered search overview, an AI-generated summary, or even an AI-created explanation inside a learning platform. They ask, “Where does this information come from?” and “What’s missing?”

Nicole

It’s important to note that AI is integrated into much of what we do now. Our students need to be critical about AI outputs when doing a Google search, using an AI-powered research tool, or using a chatbot.

Academic Goals

- Students will learn to question sources and information.
- The class will help identify and assess the accuracy and biases of AI-generated works.
- We will emphasize the *M* (monitor) in HUMAN.

Teacher Big Ideas

- This EduProtocol provides practice and guidance for developing the habit of questioning artificial intelligence (and other sources) by asking, “Is this accurate?” and “What’s missing?”
- This skill will help your students in any research they do and hopefully in life as we move forward in a world with artificial intelligence.

Kate

I teach my students how to use Perplexity AI as a research tool when we're working on research projects. This is the perfect time to use this EduProtocol. When they ask it for sources on a topic, they then run through this protocol to evaluate and verify what they find. But this protocol should be done anytime students are interacting with any AI tool when looking for factual information.

tinyurl.com/rabbitholing

Prepare for the Activity

1. Determine what AI output students will evaluate.
2. Prepare the template. (Scan the QR code or visit tinyurl.com/rabbitholing to access the Rabbit Holing template.)

The Activity

Step 1: Interact with AI

1. Share the template with students.
2. After students have generated AI output that needs evaluation, move to the template.

Name:

Original Topic/Source:

Notes from your AI interaction

Add your notes here

Note-taking guide for an AI interaction.

Step 2: Go Down the Rabbit Hole!

- Have students verify the information they learned in the AI output. They should open two to three tabs and find other sources that verify the original information, then record their findings on the template.
- Students can consider the following questions:
  - Where did the original information come from?
  - Is the information given true?
  - What evidence are you finding to back up the original information you found?

New Source:

- Where did the original information come from?
- Is the information given true?
- What evidence are you finding to back up the original information you found?

Source 1

What did you learn?

Template for the first source.

Step 3: Reflect

1. Have students share their conclusions with a partner.
2. Choose one aha moment to share with the class.

New Source:

Conclusion

What did you learn? Compare the original information to the new information you found:

Guide for the conclusion.

Suggestions for Teachers

- Model this process for your students before you do it for the first time. You can share one AI-generated output with the entire class and walk through the process together, sharing what you find along the way.

- Include your students in a conversation about bias and inaccuracies by having them share examples whenever they find them.

EduProtocol AI Power-Up: Integrating AI

If you want your students to treat AI as a thought partner, not a fact machine, SchoolAI is the ideal platform to support the Rabbit Holing EduProtocol. Its customizable Space Designer lets you preprogram AI conversations that challenge students to verify information rather than blindly accept it. For real-time inquiry and source evaluation, pair it with Perplexity, a student-friendly AI search engine that provides citations and promotes lateral reading.

Here's how SchoolAI boosts the learning:

- You can build a bot that walks students through key lateral reading questions. Where did this information come from? What might be missing? What sources would verify this?
- Instead of overwhelming students with an open-ended chat interface, you can shape the AI's behavior to encourage metacognition and skepticism, hallmarks of ethical AI use.
- With school-ready privacy policies and moderation controls, SchoolAI keeps student interactions focused, safe, and appropriate for all ages.
- Not sure how to build a bot? Use SchoolAI's Space Designer to help you!

Here's how Perplexity supports this EduProtocol:

- Students get AI-generated answers with linked sources, which helps them practice citing, tracing claims, and comparing information.
- Its "related questions" feature nudges students toward further inquiry, modeling the habits of curiosity and critical thinking.

- Perplexity isn't a static chatbot; it mirrors how students already use search engines, bridging classroom practice and real-world behavior.
- Students can evaluate the quality of cited sources and decide which ones are trustworthy, a key skill in any fact-checking activity.

With SchoolAI guiding reflective dialogue and Perplexity offering transparent, source-linked responses, both tools help build the habits of lateral reading and informed skepticism. SchoolAI and Perplexity reinforce the message that AI isn't the answer; it's the beginning of the question.

Leverage AI to Apply to Your Content

This EduProtocol is applicable across all subject areas because the core skill of questioning accuracy and verifying information is relevant to every discipline.

In any class, students can use AI to explore a concept, event, technique, or process and then practice lateral reading to confirm their understanding. Whether they are fact-checking historical claims in social studies, validating safety procedures in a CTE course, examining nutritional advice in FCS, or verifying math explanations, the process is the same:

- Interact with AI as a thought partner.
- Question the accuracy of the output.
- Use multiple trusted sources to confirm or challenge this information.
- Reflect on what was accurate, what wasn't, and why it matters.

This helps students build habits of mind that will serve them in any field: curiosity, critical thinking, and an understanding that AI, *like any source*, needs to be verified.

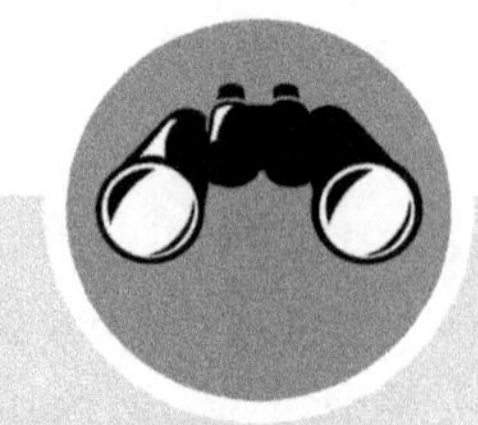

Chapter 14
Shoe Bias

It was a typical day in class. Students quietly typed away, brainstorming ideas for their podcasts. Then suddenly, someone said, "This is garbage! What the . . .?" The outburst drew my attention. I looked up to see one of my students turning her laptop screen toward me. "Ms. Meyer, can you believe this?" she said, exasperated.

Her group had been struggling to come up with a catchy name for their podcast, and I'd suggested they give an AI tool a shot. The results? Not what they were hoping for.

"All the suggestions it gave us are stuff like 'girl power,' 'sparkles,' and 'glitter'!" she said.

I asked, "What did you input?"

She read her prompt: "We are four high school girls making a podcast about the American dream . . ."

That's when it clicked—this was a teachable moment about bias in AI. The mention of "four high school girls" had steered the AI toward gendered assumptions.

That's where this EduProtocol comes in. It helps students learn to pause, evaluate AI output, spot potential biases, and ask better questions. When we guide them through this kind of process, we're not just teaching them to use AI; we're teaching them to think critically about what they get back and to make more thoughtful choices about when and how to use these tools.

HUMAN

Shoe Bias ASKING WHAT'S MISSING?

Observe + Predict + Create + Reflect

Description

Students will closely examine AI-generated outputs, becoming thoughtful and strategic thinkers. They will confront bias head-on by identifying problematic assumptions and missing perspectives and using prompts to guide AI toward more balanced outputs. Through critical observation and creative reasoning, students will fill in gaps by refining prompts and generating images that reflect diverse viewpoints.

Jon

This EduProtocol will teach the kids how to spot bias. Kids will use this skill that you give them for a lifetime.

Academic Goals

- Students will understand that AI can have a biased output.
- The class will evaluate AI outputs and create a new output based on missing pieces.

Teacher Big Ideas

- This EduProtocol helps students understand that AI is a tool and can be biased. Bias needs to be met head-on, and one way to do that is by prompting.

Prepare for the Activity

1. Choose an image generation tool. You'll need a tool that can create three images from a single prompt. Pick one that's accessible to you and your students (for example: Adobe Firefly, Canva, or Padlet—ChatGPT will also do this, but please note that it's only available to users thirteen and older who have permission).
2. Decide on a one-word or simple phrase prompt. Select a term or phrase that will produce a set of images with potential for discussion about bias or missing perspectives. Examples: shoes, house, scientist, doctor, dentist, veterinarian, librarian, nurse, beauty, family, professional.
3. Generate the images. These images will be placed into the first three boxes of your template. You might ask it to generate all three images at once: "Create three separate images of shoes," or "Create three separate images of a house." If you'd like, you can generate multiple sets of images to offer student choice during the activity.
4. Create a slide template. Use our Shoe Bias template or create your own.
5. Scan the QR code or visit tinyurl.com/shoebias to access the Shoe Bias template.

Kate

I have done this with great success using *nurse* and *doctor*. There are often some glaring biases that show through that the students are quick to pick up on.

tinyurl.com/shoebias

The Activity

Step 1: Observe

Have students look at the first three filled boxes and observe. What do they notice?

Here are two different examples: shoes and houses.

Step 2: Predict

- Students think about what logically fits in the missing fourth box.
- They ask, "What's missing? What perspectives, people, or ideas are left out? What assumptions have been made?"

Step 3: Create

1. Students create a prompt that will generate a fourth image. This image should be the answer to the questions in step 2.
2. Have students generate the image and adjust as needed. Add it to the template with the final prompt.

PROMPT: Please create a pair of sandals that are worn and well-loved. They are comfortable yet practical. The purpose of the shoes is to wear them during warm months. They should be women's shoes that are pretty but have no heel.

Add the fourth image with the prompt.

Marlena

This is a reminder that teaching critical thinking about AI isn't just about the tech; it's about empathy, awareness, and ensuring that every voice gets a seat at the table.

Step 4: Reflect and Discuss

Have students share and explain their choice with a partner or group.

- Compare answers—did others have different ideas that also make sense?
- Ask, "How does recognizing missing perspectives help us challenge bias in AI and the world?"

Suggestions for Teachers

- Bias gets highlighted or ignored in content, framing, and representation. Using the question "What's missing?" helps students detect hidden biases and prompt AI to fill in the gaps.
- Encourage students to ask, "What's missing?" in all the work they're doing.

- After the EduProtocol is completed, you could challenge students to give the images to a chatbot and ask it to describe the bias in the images. It will often pick up on things humans might have missed! Have students compare their findings to AI's findings.

UNDERSTAND: WHERE BIAS CREEPS IN

BIAS IN TRAINING DATA

LLMs learn from the text they are fed during training. If they are fed biased or prejudiced content for training, then the model might pick up these biases. For instance, if an LLM is trained on text where it is more common for men to be in leadership positions and women to be in caregiving positions, the model may learn this association.

ABSENCE OF DIVERSE DATA

If the training data is not diverse enough and is a collection of only one group's perspective, then the model will miss out on how to fairly treat inputs from groups who are underrepresented in it; if most of the training data comes from Western sources, a model trained on it may not understand cultural references or viewpoints from other parts of the world.

HUMAN INFLUENCE

Humans, when creating and tuning these models, can allow their own unconscious biases to slip into the model. If a team working on the model has some biases, they may influence how a model will be trained and evaluated.

ALGORITHMIC CHOICES

The design of the algorithms themselves – that is, the algorithms used to train and then make the LLM models work – can introduce bias. Some technical decisions may accidentally favor one group over another. For example, if the algorithm puts different weight on some types of data, this might skew the model's answers in a biased direction.

EduProtocol AI Power-Up: Integrating AI

If you want your students to reflect on bias in AI outputs while also learning from one another's perspectives, Padlet is a powerful addition to this EduProtocol. It creates a shared visual gallery where bias isn't just discussed—it's *seen* and *challenged* collaboratively. To take it even further, pair Padlet with MagicSchool's MagicStudent, which allows students to prompt the AI to reflect on their own work or explain how bias may have shown up in generated content.

Here's how Padlet strengthens the experience:

- Each group or student can use Padlet's AI image generator on the Padlet wall. They can also use their favorite image generator (Canva, Adobe Firefly, etc.) and upload the results.
- Padlet lets everyone see how different students interpreted the same missing perspective, sparking great discussions around diversity, assumptions, and framing.
- Students can respond to each other's images using the comment feature.

Here's how MagicStudent supports deeper reflection:

- Students can use the AI Literacy Bot to examine how and why bias may appear in an AI-generated image or prompt.
- After they have done their own reflection, prompt students to ask the AI questions like these: "What assumptions might be present in this image?" or "Whose perspective might be missing here?" They can then compare their thoughts with the AI output.

Padlet and MagicStudent help students move beyond surface-level engagement to truly interrogate AI. They're not just identifying bias; they're learning how to spot it, talk about it, and think critically about their own digital choices.

Leverage AI to Apply to Your Content

Here are some ways you can apply this EduProtocol to specific subject areas.

ELA

AI generates three images: "heroes," "troublemakers," or "protagonists."

Math

AI generates three-word problems about "budgeting," "shopping," or "saving for a goal," featuring students' first names.

Science

AI generates three images of "clean energy solutions," "a scientist," or "a field researcher."

Social Studies

AI generates three images of "political leaders," "protestors," or "journalists."

Art

AI generates three images of "beautiful landscapes," "modern art," "talented musicians," or "relaxing music."

Computer Science/Digital Literacy

AI generates three images of "a programmer," "a hacker," or "a CEO."

Wood/Metal Shop

AI generates three images of "a skilled craftsperson," "a shop student," or "a shop safety poster."

Foods

AI generates three images of "a chef," "a home cook," or "a healthy meal."

Advisory/Life Skills

AI generates three images of "a student leader," "a student who needs support," or "a successful student."

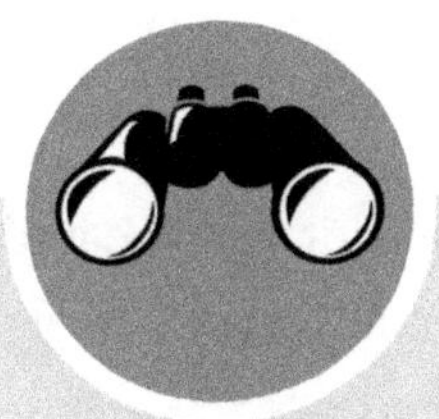

Chapter 15
Frayer: Monitor AI Like a Pro Remix

It started with a confused look.

We were doing a quick research warm-up when I asked the class, "Has AI ever given you an answer that seemed a little too perfect? Like, you don't quite trust it?"

One student raised her hand slowly. "I asked it for a quote from Maya Angelou about education," she said. "It gave me this amazing line. It was seriously beautiful, but I couldn't find it anywhere else. Not even on Google."

Another student looked up. "Wait . . . so did she say it or not?"

"She didn't," I said. "That's called a hallucination. AI made it up."

There was a beat of silence, and then someone said what a lot of them were thinking: "That's kinda scary."

"It can be," I replied, "but it doesn't have to be. The key is learning how to spot when it happens and what to do next."

That was our launching point. We talked about how AI generates texts based on patterns, not facts. How it can sound right while being totally wrong. And how important it is to double-check the details, especially when you're using AI to help with writing, research, or anything that needs to be accurate.

They were hooked. And I knew they were ready to dive into the deeper stuff: not just hallucination but bias, missing perspectives, and lateral reading, the skills that help us monitor AI with a critical lens.

To help them organize their thinking, I brought out a classic: the Frayer Model. This activity may be helpful when first discussing how to monitor AI, or it can offer students the opportunity to bring together skills they've been practicing.

"This time," I told them, "we're not using it for vocabulary. You're using it to figure out what these ideas really mean, how they show up in AI, and what to do about it."

They rolled their eyes (because they always do that to start), but a few minutes in, they were already asking sharper questions. They started noticing problems, suggesting fixes, and digging into examples on their own.

By the end of the period, they weren't just talking about hallucination and bias. They were spotting it. Explaining it. Monitoring it.

Jon

Really, calling out inaccuracies is just a skill extension of the classic Northwest tree octopus lesson or the "Abraham Lincoln invented the internet" meme. It's not a new education concern, just a new wrapper that we need to teach kids about.

The moment students realize that AI can make things up or confidently present biased information, they need a way to process it. They need tools that help them slow down, question what they're seeing, and build their own understanding of these complex concepts. That's where the Frayer Model comes in.

It's more than a vocabulary organizer in this context; it becomes a framework for ethical thinking. Instead of just memorizing definitions of *bias* or *hallucination*, students use the Frayer Model to explore where these issues show up in AI, how they can recognize them, and what they should do when they spot them.

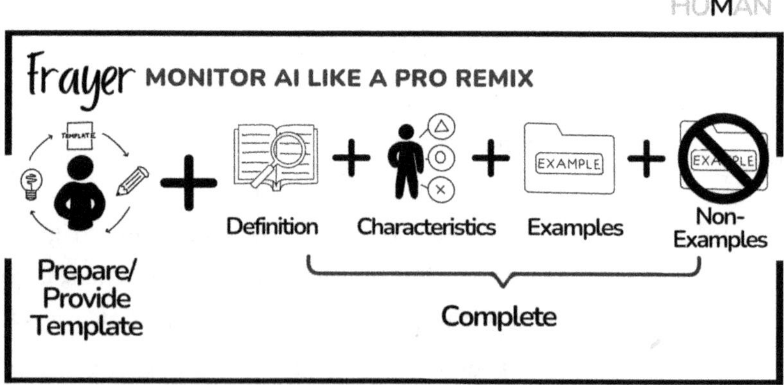

Description

The Frayer Model, a graphic organizer for building student vocabulary, helps students unpack complex or abstract concepts by breaking them into four approachable parts: definition, characteristics, examples, and non-examples. When applied to the monitor step of the HUMAN framework, this EduProtocol becomes a powerful tool for helping students understand what it means to evaluate AI outputs critically.

This EduProtocol is effective at the start of any unit where AI will be utilized for writing, research, or creative tasks, or early in the year—in fact, you may use this EduProtocol before you use others in this chapter. It lays the groundwork for the ethical and informed monitoring of AI, providing students with an EduProtocol they can refer to repeatedly.

Marlena

Dorothy Frayer was a genius when she invented the Frayer Model, but I bet she had no idea it would someday be used to help students understand generative AI!

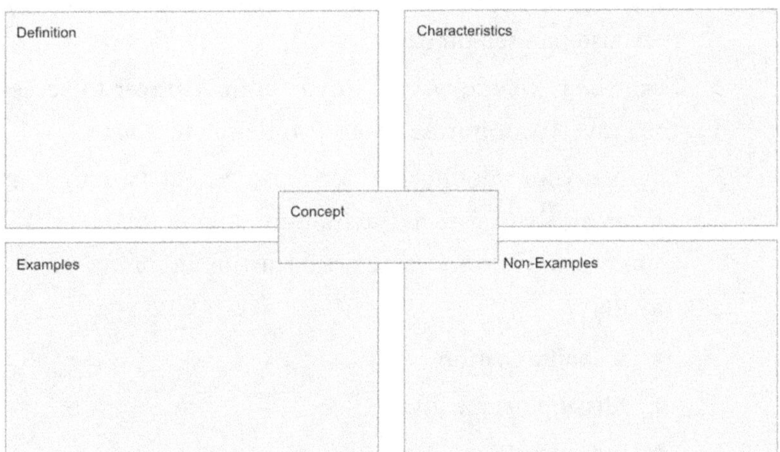

The Frayer Model.

Academic Goals

- Students will develop a deeper understanding of key monitoring concepts (bias, hallucination, missing perspectives, and lateral reading).

- The class will build critical thinking and media literacy skills.
- We will apply responsible monitoring strategies.

Teacher Big Ideas

- This EduProtocol makes abstract concepts visible. Bias and hallucinations can feel vague or overwhelming to students, but the Frayer Model breaks them down in a concrete way.
- It's a conversation starter, not just a graphic organizer.
- It builds habits that students carry into every AI interaction.

Prepare for the Activity

1. Prepare the Frayer Model in an electronic format (Frayer may also be used on paper).
2. Scan the QR code or visit tinyurl.com/AIfrayer to access the Frayer: Monitor AI Like a Pro Remix template.
3. Choose your monitoring concepts. Select two to four key terms that relate to the monitor step of the HUMAN framework. Here are some great starting points:
    - Bias
    - AI hallucination
    - Missing perspectives
    - Inaccuracies
    - Lateral reading

Depending on your goals and class size, you can assign one term per group, allow students to choose, or give everyone the same term. This goes in the "Concept" box of the template.

tinyurl.com/AIfrayer

The Activity

Step 1: Template

Provide a copy of the Frayer template to each student or pair of students if working in teams. (Frayers are commonly used individually but may be used with partners to extend the value of concept construction through collaboration and conversation.)

Step 2: Frayer Activity

Students complete the Frayer using words and images. You can guide them with these prompts if they need them:

- Definition: What does this word mean in your own words, especially when talking about AI?
- Characteristics: What are the signs that this is happening in an AI response? How can you tell?
- Examples: When have you seen this happen? What's a real or possible scenario where this might show up?
- Non-Examples: What seems similar but isn't the same thing? What's a common misunderstanding?

Step 3: Optional Extension

Ask students to include a visual metaphor or image that represents the concept.

Step 4: Gallery Walk

Once the Frayers are complete, students participate in a quick gallery walk, digital slide share, or pair-and-compare activity to discuss their findings. Encourage them to look for these:

- Surprising examples
- Different interpretations of the same term
- Creative image choices
- Patterns in how these show up in AI

Step 5: Optional Exit Ticket

Ask students, "What did someone else write that extended your thinking or made you think differently about your own term?"

Suggestions for Teachers

- The Frayer Model is one of the most flexible tools in your teaching toolbox. While it's often used to support vocabulary development, its real power lies in helping students unpack layered, nuanced, or abstract concepts, especially those they need to internalize, not memorize. Asking students to define a term, identify its characteristics, provide examples, and offer non-examples requires more than just a quick Google search. It pushes them to connect the concept to their own understanding and context.
- Whether students are evaluating a piece of writing, analyzing a historical event, explaining a scientific process, or designing a creative project, the Frayer Model helps them pause, think deeper, and engage more meaningfully with the content you're teaching.

EduProtocol AI Power-Up: Integrating AI

Snorkl is the perfect tool to scaffold students' thinking when using the Frayer: Monitor AI Like a Pro Remix EduProtocol. Even better, Snorkl has the Frayer EduProtocol built right into its platform, making this a seamless plug-and-play option. Pair Snorkl with Class Companion, an AI-powered platform that offers personalized, rubric-aligned feedback and self-reflection prompts based on your learning goals to deepen the learning loop.

Here's how Snorkl strengthens this EduProtocol:

- Some EduProtocols are built right into Snorkl, and Frayer is one of them! Simply use the template Snorkl has created and get up and running in seconds!

- After getting Snorkl's feedback, students can revise their definitions or examples, strengthening both their content understanding and communication skills.
- You can align this task with specific learning goals so students get feedback tied directly to your Frayer quadrants.

Here's how Class Companion supports this EduProtocol:

- Students receive immediate AI-generated feedback with opportunities for self-reflection built right in.
- Use Class Companion for the exit ticket extension of this EduProtocol to get students reflecting even deeper!

Snorkl and Class Companion turn the Frayer: Monitor AI Like a Pro Remix EduProtocol into a dynamic feedback loop. Students don't just define; they clarify, revise, and reflect. It's how we move from surface-level understanding to expert-level thinking, powered by AI!

SECTION 5
Authenticate Through Inquiry

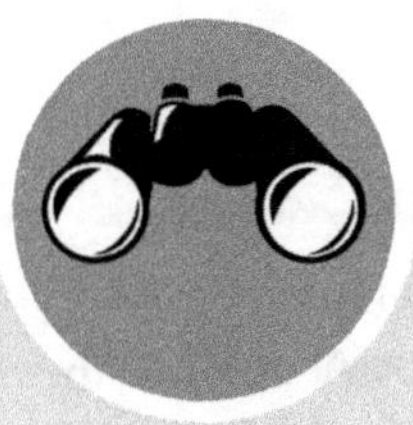

Chapter 16
HUMAN: Authenticate

In this new age of AI, the line between using a tool to help versus to do the task has gotten a lot harder to see. Tools like ChatGPT can write essays, solve problems, and generate content in seconds, which raises new questions for all of us about what counts as authentic student work. This is where *authenticate*, the *A* in our HUMAN framework, comes in. Let's focus on rethinking our approach to academic honesty and establishing clear, realistic expectations for the ethical use of AI in the classroom. This step of the HUMAN framework teaches students that they can use AI without sacrificing authenticity.

Through conversations with my students, I have learned that they care deeply about doing the right thing. In a class reflection, my juniors shared that they *want* to use AI ethically, and they look to us to show them how.

Teach students how to use AI ethically. Many students use AI and not many of them know how to use it ethically, but if they are educated on how to use it they will realize that AI can be used as an assistant to help them with their own thoughts and not have AI do things completely for them.
I don't use it but I think its important to note that AI isn't inherently evil entity trying to lie and cheat, it is a tool, it's how students use it and how different ones are programed thats concerning, and as teachers and adults, it your responsibility to teach and understand the tool and how not to use it as such.

That AI isn't the enemy and it is super helpful for a lot of students Most students aren't going to purposefully use AI unethically because students don't want to feel guilty or like they're cheating. Of course, some students will use their resources unethically but that's how it's always been even before AI existed. AI helps students who learn at different or slower paces by letting them be able to summarize, take notes, etc way easier than before.

We don't all use it. If we use it it isn't always for cheating or plagiarism. Most of us have as many questions about it as you.

Some of my students' reflections on AI in the classroom.

This was an important insight that shaped my approach to integrating AI tools into our learning environment. Rather than assuming students would misuse these tools, I realized I needed to guide them in using AI responsibly and transparently within our academic framework.

We also ground our AI usage in consent. OpenAI requires explicit parental consent for users under eighteen, so I sent home permission slips outlining how we'd use AI in class. This was part of a larger effort to create a culture of trust and shared responsibility. To my delight, I received a 100 percent return rate, and the conversations with parents reinforced the importance of thoughtful AI integration.

When addressing plagiarism, the default reaction is often to focus on detection. However, AI plagiarism detectors are unreliable and can disproportionately flag non-native English speakers. Other strategies, like using extensions to track drafts in Google Docs, are helpful but only offer part of the solution. And while paper-and-pencil methods might seem like a safe alternative, relying on them exclusively risks undermining accommodations that some students need to thrive.

The better response? Build a classroom culture where AI use is openly discussed, ethically practiced, and guided. Here's how:

Marlena

The *why* makes all the difference; it's the bigger picture that helps students understand AI's role and make thoughtful, responsible choices about how they use it.

1. Be clear from the start. Just like I did with my letter home and class conversations, make sure students know what's okay (and what's not) when it comes to AI use.
2. Teach the *why*, not just the rules. Help students think about ethical AI use—not just as a way to avoid cheating but as a way to grow as learners.
3. Build in reflection. Encourage students to pause and think about how and why they're using AI and whether it's helping them learn or doing the work for them.

I often take on the role of co-learner with my students when discussing plagiarism in the age of AI. Because of the culture of transparency that I create in my classroom about AI use, my students often come to me with questions about using AI in different contexts. They'll often show me their prompts and output and ask, "If I do this [take this suggestion, use this wording, make these changes], is it plagiarism?" I like to ask them, "If you took this paper to Mr. L for feedback, and he made those suggestions and you used them, would that be ethical?" or "If you had a friend help you and they offered that same feedback and you used it, would it be ethical?" We talk through this together. I do not presume to have the ultimate answer, which helps my students think through their use of AI.

Ultimately, our role as educators is not to ban AI but to harness it as a tool for growth and creativity. By modifying our expectations and personalizing our approach, we can teach students how to navigate these new technologies responsibly, ensuring they see AI not as a shortcut but as a tool for learning. The three EduProtocols in this chapter are designed to help you achieve this goal.

Nicole

Regardless of where you are with your students' use of AI, you need to provide them with clear expectations for AI use.

Jon

More things, faster. Less work for teachers. More creation, comparing, and discernment for kids. This is why we have to change our teaching style.

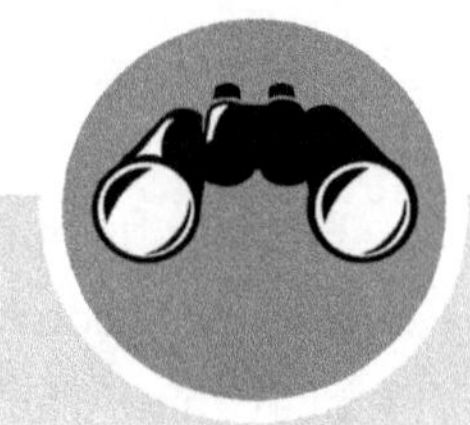

Chapter 17
Pop-Up AI

POP-UP AI

The music video plays, and suddenly—*pop!*—a little bubble appears on the screen. "This scene took fourteen hours to film." *Pop!* "The lead singer sprained his ankle during this take." *Pop!* "The budget for this music video was bigger than the cost of the band's first album."

In the late 1990s and early 2000s, *Pop-Up Video* was a must-watch for anyone with a television and a love for music videos. VH1 took the songs we knew by heart and layered them with trivia, behind-the-scenes gossip, and random but fascinating facts. It was like falling down a Wikipedia rabbit hole of information before Wikipedia existed, only instead of clicking, the facts popped right up on the screen, allowing you to experience the music video in a whole new way.

Back then, this felt like the future. Could technology do this? Layer information onto something familiar, making it richer, deeper, and more interesting? It was like someone had cracked open a secret vault of knowledge and delivered it to our screens in real time.

Just like *Pop-Up Video* added layers of insight to a music video, this EduProtocol does the same for student work, only instead of fun facts about celebrity mishaps, the pop-ups capture deep thinking and metacognitive reflection. With each pop-up, students peel back the layers of their own thinking, identifying what feels authentic and what needs revision. It's not just about using AI—it's about making AI work for them, ensuring that the final product accurately reflects their ideas, not just a polished-up output.

HUMAN

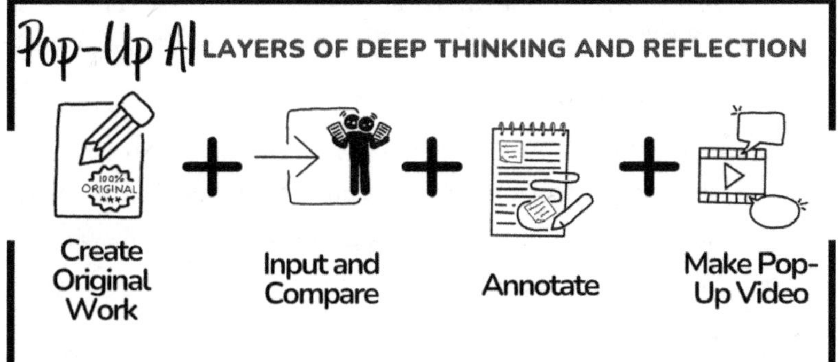

Description

Students will critically analyze and reflect on AI-generated content by evaluating how it enhances, alters, or misinterprets their original ideas. Learners will create a VH1-style pop-up video to engage in metacognition about AI's role in creative work.

Marlena

Use this EduProtocol throughout the year. As your students' understanding of content expands, so will their mastery of AI tools and prompts.

Academic Goals

- Students will develop metacognitive skills and reflect on the creative process.
- The class will learn how AI tools can alter, enhance, or misrepresent ideas.
- Students will strengthen their creative confidence and find a voice in their work with AI as a collaborator.
- We will practice ethical AI use, transparency, and ownership.

Teacher Big Ideas

- AI should be a thought partner, not a ghostwriter. This EduProtocol models healthy boundaries around AI use by demonstrating how students can transform, critique, and reflect on AI outputs, rather than simply accepting them.

- Reflection is the key to authentic AI use. The pop-up format makes the invisible visible; students' reflections demonstrate deeper learning and responsible engagement with technology.
- Voice and identity still matter in the age of AI. By comparing their work with AI outputs, students discover what makes their ideas and voice unique, a key takeaway in any AI-integrated classroom.

Prepare for the Activity

1. Select the type of original work the students will use for this activity (poetry, script, analysis, instructions, review, podcast outline, images, etc.). You might also decide to let the students choose.
2. Select the AI tool(s) you want your students to use (LLM for text, an image generator or AI music tool, a podcast planner, etc.). Test it in advance to understand how it behaves with student input.

The Activity

Step 1: Create Original Work

Students begin by developing their original ideas in one of the following formats (this serves as their creative foundation before engaging with AI):

- A song or poem
- An image
- A script
- A podcast outline
- Anything else!

Step 2: Input Work into an AI Tool

Students use an AI-powered tool to transform their original work into an AI-generated version. Here are examples of AI tools:

- LLMs for scripts
- Song creators for music
- Image generators for visuals
- Podcast outline makers for structured discussion

Step 3: Extract and Compare

Students retrieve the AI-generated version of their work and compare it to their original.

Step 4: Reflect

- Students critically analyze the AI's output, answering key questions. These annotations will appear as overlays in their final video, mimicking the classic VH1 *Pop-Up Video* style. Here are the questions:
  - What did the AI get right?
  - What did the AI enhance?
  - What did the AI miss?
  - Where do you see your original work coming through?
  - What part of this is AI-generated?
  - Are you proud of this? Why or why not?
- Encourage students to note the limitations of AI and how they might refine the output.
- If you want to try out the template, scan the QR code or visit tinyurl.com/AIpopup to access the Pop-Up AI template.

tinyurl.com/AIpopup

Kate

This is a great place to pull out the ROBOT framework again! Students can prompt AI to make changes to their original. Give them time to play and explore all the different outputs they'll get with different prompts.

Nicole

It's important to remember that if you choose to use a tool without a clear data privacy agreement—one that explicitly states it does not collect or store user data (check with your tech department)—there's a chance that anything entered into the AI could be used to train the system. This possibility should be clearly communicated to students (or to parents, depending on the students' age). Additionally, students should be taught never to input personally identifiable information (PII) into any AI system. This includes names, addresses, or any other details that could identify them.

Step 5: Introduce Pop-Up Concept

Search for VH1 *Pop-Up Video* on YouTube for some original models! Watch them together and discuss what you see. This will help define what this format is.

Step 6: Create a VH1-Style Pop-Up Video

- Students compile their original and AI-generated work into a video format, embedding their reflection pop-ups throughout. The template includes some possible formats that can be used for this step.
- They can record themselves discussing key insights.
- Pop-ups should appear at relevant moments in the video to highlight their thoughts.
- The final video serves as both a reflection and a creative showcase.

Check out the pop-up example here.

Suggestions for Teachers

- Even though pop-up videos are the original inspiration for this activity, don't stress about the technology and creating a video. The final product is great, but ultimately, it's the learning that is important. Students could do this with a slide deck and some animation.
- If you're unsure how to create the video, consider asking your school's tech staff or searching for a YouTube tutorial. Canva is also a great way to make this happen; it's very easy, and your students will be able to figure it out and help one another.

Kate

Canva has video templates that make this work easy. Don't worry if you don't feel like you're an expert; let the students figure it out!

Nicole

This EduProtocol doesn't necessarily need a template. The template we are providing gives some pop-ups that your students could fill in. I created an example of a poem I wrote, annotated, and put into AI. I reflected on what was done using this EduProtocol. I'm also including a video in the template that demonstrates how to create a pop-up video using Canva to help you through this process.

Kate

Back in the early 2000s, I used to do a version of this on a poster board that I called Pop-Up Poetry.

EduProtocol AI Power-Up: Integrating AI

Class Companion helps students go deeper with metacognition, which is the heart of this EduProtocol. While it doesn't generate pop-up videos, it's the perfect preproduction partner, helping students analyze, refine, and reflect *before* they hit record. Then, to bring those reflections to life, Canva steps in as a student-friendly design platform for building dynamic, multimedia-rich pop-up presentations.

Here's how Class Companion supports Pop-Up AI:

- Students can upload the text of both their original and AI-transformed work and receive structured feedback prompts that mirror your pop-up questions.
- Students can revise their reflections based on the suggestions, helping them clarify and deepen their commentary before embedding it into video form.
- If you want to scaffold this for students, you can customize prompts so their pop-ups are first drafted as thoughtful written responses.

Here's how Canva brings it to life:

- Students can layer text pop-ups over images and add music, animations, and transitions, all in a drag-and-drop interface that feels intuitive and fun.
- Canva is the perfect tool for creating short, polished multimedia presentations that embed reflections in an engaging and easy-to-share format.

With Class Companion guiding the critical thinking and Canva powering the creative expression, Pop-Up AI becomes a meaningful blend of analysis and artistry. Together, they help students explain their thinking *and* showcase it with style.

Leverage AI to Apply to Your Content

The EduProtocol is a flexible, cross-curricular strategy that works in any subject area where students produce original work. Whether they're writing an essay, solving a math problem, analyzing historical events, composing music, or designing an art piece, students use AI as a creative partner, not a shortcut. By comparing their original work with an AI-generated version, students engage in deep reflection through pop-up annotations that highlight what the AI got right, what it misunderstood, and how students' thinking comes through. This process promotes ethical use of AI, reinforces student voice and authorship, and builds critical thinking as students learn to revise, refine, and reclaim their work from AI's influence.

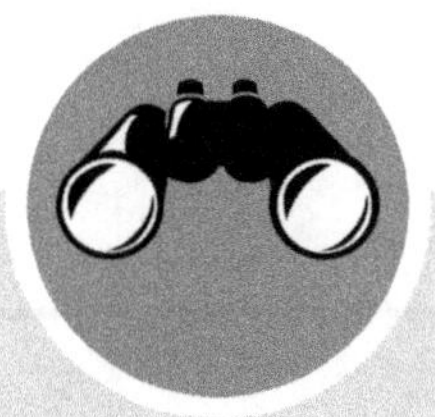

Chapter 18
AI Chopped: Slang Showdown

AI CHOPPED

One of my favorite ways to start a new course is a quick dive into generational studies. Not the dry, textbook kind. This is more about laughing together to set the tone for the semester. I tell them, "I'm Gen X. You're Gen Z. Let's talk about what that means."

We discuss pop culture, trends, and, of course, slang. I confess to them that when I hear words like *delulu*, *gyatt*, or *rizz*, my brain sometimes goes blank. Meanwhile, when I toss out gems from my own teen years, like *rad*, *gnarly*, and *wack*, they just shake their heads.

And that's when we discuss something more profound: Language isn't static. It shifts and morphs with each generation. Slang isn't just about being trendy. It's about identity, community, and voice. It's about making language your own.

It's the perfect lead-in to our AI Chopped: Slang Showdown EduProtocol. In this activity, students will take class content and remix it into creative slang. But there's a twist: They'll be using AI tools. Carefully. Intentionally. They'll practice the *A* (authenticate) from the HUMAN framework. Because in a world of AI-generated everything, learning to put your stamp on your work matters more than ever.

And along the way? We'll all be laughing a lot!

Marlena

That right there is, like, totally bodacious!

Jon

This isn't a cooking show!

HUMAN

Description

In this EduProtocol, students compete in the AI Slang Chopped Kitchen, using artificial intelligence to translate course concepts into peer-legible slang. Students may apply existing slang they already use or invent new slang-style phrases, as long as the meaning stays clear and connected to the content.

Each team is assigned a different AI use level, which shapes how they interact with the AI to complete this task. Across all levels, students must evaluate, verify, and translate back into academic language to prove their understanding. The focus of this EduProtocol is the authenticate step of the HUMAN framework: Students are not trying to hide AI use; they're learning how to transform AI output into something accurate, appropriate, and unmistakably their own.

Academic Goals

- Students will deepen content understanding by translating content-specific concepts into peer-legible slang (student voice) while preserving accurate meaning.
- The class will practice ethical and intentional use of AI by working within a clearly defined AI use level.

- Learners will develop skills in prompting, evaluating, and revising AI-generated content responsibly.
- We will reflect on authorship, voice, and ownership in AI-assisted work, including transparent labeling of what was generated, revised, or created independently.

Teacher Big Ideas

- Not all AI use is equal; students need guided experiences across a spectrum and models of what different uses look like.
- Authentic work isn't about hiding AI but transforming its output into something accurate, meaningful, and clearly created by students.
- Critical thinking and student voice should be part of the final products. Students should be able to translate their slang back into academic language to prove comprehension.

Prepare for the Activity

1. Select two to four course concepts that students already understand at a basic level. This EduProtocol works best as a review because students need enough familiarity to judge whether the slang is accurate.
2. Select an AI tool. Pick one that students can use for generating ideas (MagicSchool's MagicStudent is a great choice for this activity—try the Idea Generator tool.).
3. Prepare the template. Each team gets one slide.
4. Scan the QR code or visit tinyurl.com/AIchopped to access the AI Chopped template.

tinyurl.com/AIchopped

The Activity

Step 1: Groups

Divide the students into four teams and assign each team a specific AI usage level:

- **No AI Nibbler (no AI):** This team must create slang and definitions from scratch. No AI is allowed.
- **Thoughtful Tinkerers (AI as a thought partner):** This team can use AI in the initial brainstorming only (ideas, lists, examples). After that, the slang and definitions must be rewritten in student voice to make it authentically theirs.
- **Back-and-Forth Bakers (AI collaborators):** This team can interact with AI as much as they want, but all progress must happen through iterative prompting and revising. Their work should show evidence of decision-making: choices, edits, and refinements.
- **Prompt-and-Go Pastry Chefs (AI first draft):** This team may enter *one* prompt and use the AI output as is, without edits.

Nicole

These groups will move at different speeds. Group 4 looks "done" quickly, but their real work is prompt quality. Remind them that one prompt doesn't mean one minute. It means one shot. Their time should be spent crafting the prompt to get the best output.

Step 2: Content and Rules

- Review the content if needed (especially key vocabulary or misunderstandings you've noticed).
- Set the ground rules for slang (adjust for grade level):
    - Keep it school appropriate.
    - Respect all voices.
    - Keep it clear and connected to the content.
    - Have fun, but be ready to explain the real meaning.

Step 3: Slang Creations and Brainstorming

1. All teams create a list of two to four slang terms or phrases that explain the selected content concepts (two is a great starting point).
2. For each slang term, students complete the template:
   - They choose a slang word or phrase.
   - They write down what concept it explains.
   - They explain why they chose this slang for this academic concept.
3. Students examine their slang terms or phrases using the questions at the top of the template:
   - Is it accurate to the concept?
   - Is it peer legible (something my classmates would understand)?
   - Is it school appropriate?
   - How can I revise this to make it more personal, clear, or accurate?

AI CHOPPED GROUP 1

- ❑ Is it accurate to the concept?
- ❑ Is it peer legible (something my classmates would understand)?
- ❑ Is it school appropriate?

If all of these are not checked off, revise your slang word or phrase and think about how you can make it more personal, clear, or accurate.

Slang Word or Phrase:	Slang Word or Phrase:	Slang Word or Phrase:	Slang Word or Phrase:
What concept does it explain:	What concept does it explain:	What concept does it explain:	What concept does it explain:
Explanation:	Explanation:	Explanation:	Explanation:

Step 4: Slang Showdown!

1. Each team chooses their best slang term or phrase and puts it on the Final Group Selection slide along with the concept it explains and the explanation.
2. As a class, vote on the best slang term or phrase.

AI CHOPPED
GROUP 1

- ❑ Is it accurate to the concept?
- ❑ Is it peer legible (something my classmates would understand)?
- ❑ Is it school appropriate?

If all of these are not checked off, revise your slang word or phrase and think about how you can make it more personal, clear, or accurate.

Slang Word or Phrase:	Slang Word or Phrase:	Slang Word or Phrase:	Slang Word or Phrase:
What concept does it explain:	What concept does it explain:	What concept does it explain:	What concept does it explain:
Explanation:	Explanation:	Explanation:	Explanation:

Step 5: The Reveal

- Students disclose their level of AI use.
  - Here are some discussion questions:
  - What surprised you (or what did you notice) about the winning slang term or phrase?
  - How did you feel about completing the task based on your group's AI use level?

Suggestions for Teachers

- Sometimes it's fun to lean into the theme. Start the lesson by saying, "Today, you're culinary creators, and your task is to cook up the freshest, most creative slang for [insert your content]. But there's a twist: Your kitchen rules depend on how you're allowed to use AI."

- Make sure each team understands their AI usage level. Provide the template slide that outlines what is allowed and what isn't for their role.
- Have sample prompts ready for the AI-first and AI-collaborator groups. This helps students craft effective, content-rich prompts while staying focused on learning.
- Keep the spotlight on originality and learning. Remind students that the best "dish" isn't the one with the flashiest slang—it's the one that shows the deepest understanding and most ethical, thoughtful creation.

EduProtocol AI Power-Up: Integrating AI

If you want a great extension opportunity, Canva is the ultimate remix tool. It lets students pair their slang definitions with graphics, videos, music, or even mini commercials. It also gives them ownership over tone and authorship, mirroring how voice is shaped across media. You could also try layering in Snorkl and Class Companion, two AI tools that sharpen student writing by promoting revision, clarity, and intentionality. Try all three tools, or just one, and see how engaged your students become with AI!

Here's how Canva fuels this EduProtocol:

- After drafting their slang definitions, students use Canva to turn their final version into an ad, meme, skit, or animated explainer. This requires them to understand tone deeply and spot when AI's tone doesn't match their intent.
- Students can present a split-screen version—AI version on one side, remix on the other—to invite discussion on who the real author is.

Here's how Snorkl strengthens this protocol:

- After drafting, students can use Snorkl's feedback to check for tone, clarity, and effective use of language.

- Revision becomes purposeful. Students aren't just correcting grammar but enhancing authenticity and audience awareness.

Here's how Class Companion supports deeper reflection:

- Students receive targeted feedback and have the chance to reflect or revise before presenting their final showdown version.
- This tool helps students evaluate not just what's funny or catchy but what's effective in meeting the rhetorical challenge.

Leveling up with these AI-powered tools makes AI Chopped: Slang Showdown more than a writing challenge; it becomes a full-cycle learning experience. These tools work together to make students not just creators but intentional communicators.

Leverage AI to Apply to Your Content

The AI Chopped: Slang Showdown EduProtocol is a playful, powerful way to deepen understanding across any subject area. Whether students are breaking down scientific terms, translating historical ideas, or reimagining literary concepts, this activity allows them to engage in thoughtful, creative expression, layered with intentional AI use. By applying different levels of AI interaction, students practice ethical decision-making, learn to evaluate the quality of AI outputs, and revise work to reflect their voice and understanding. The focus isn't on the flashiest slang but on whether students can explain what they created, how AI contributed, and how they made it authentically theirs. These are all key elements of the authenticate principle from the HUMAN framework. Here are some additional extension options:

- Compile a class "slang dictionary" of your content.
- Challenge yourself to do this with different pop culture elements, such as hashtags or memes.

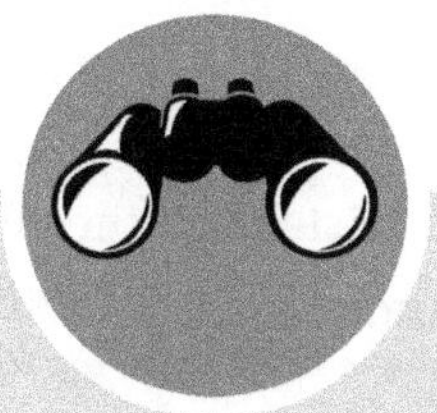

Chapter 19
Cyber Sandwich: Thought Fuel Remix

I used to think plagiarism was a simple concept.

Copying someone else's work equals cheating. End of story.

Then, generative AI emerged, and suddenly that equation became muddied. Now a student can type a prompt into ChatGPT, get a solid idea, rewrite it in their own voice, and still be left wondering, "Is this mine? Did I cheat?"

And they aren't wondering in secret. They're asking. They're not trying to get away with something but trying to get it right. They want to make sure their work is authentic.

During a writing workshop where students were working on writing editorials, one of them came over to my table and asked, completely seriously, "If I ask AI to help me with my claim and it gives me a good one, is that cheating?"

Before I could answer, someone called out from across the room, "Wait, what if I write it and then ask AI to fix the grammar. Is that cheating or just being smart?" I heard a few kids giggle, but really, they were all waiting to hear what I would say.

Marlena

How is this different from when I researched a topic in our family set of *Britannica* encyclopedias and then rewrote a paragraph in my own words? And let's be honest, sometimes I hardly understood it to begin with!

Jon

Questions and dialogue like this are why we Smart Start. We've already built creativity and trust into the classroom. You won't get the same discourse by launching straight into the academic task.

Another asked, "Okay, but what if I just stare at the blank screen for an hour and then get desperate and ask AI for help? Is that a crime or just survival?"

Cue the laughter. And the nods.

What struck me most wasn't the content of their questions. It was the tone. They were curious. Thoughtful. Sincere. They weren't trying to cut corners; they were trying to figure out the new rules of authorship.

That's what inspired this EduProtocol.

It's not enough to just tell them the rules. I wanted to give them a space to wrestle with these gray areas together, compare ideas, ask hard questions, and start building their own sense of ethical AI use. And because my students like to talk things out with a partner, I reached for one of my favorite discussion-and-synthesis EduProtocols: Cyber Sandwich.

In the context of AI and academic honesty, Cyber Sandwich serves as a means for students to navigate ethical dilemmas through conversation. They're not just being handed a list of rules. Instead, they're exploring real-life situations, discussing them, and forming their own opinions about how AI can be used responsibly.

This lesson helps with that. Instead of standing at the front of the room giving a talk about plagiarism, you get to hand the conversation over to them. They read. They talk. They ask each other questions. And in the process, they begin to figure out where they stand.

HUMAN

CyberSandwich THOUGHT FUEL REMIX

Read the Source + Discuss and Report Findings + Write

Description

Cyber Sandwich is a partner-based EduProtocol designed to help students move beyond passive reading or copy-paste thinking. It's built around structured collaboration. Each student explores a source (text, image, video, podcast, or something else), takes notes, and then comes together with others to compare what stood out to each of them. After the conversation, they each write a short paragraph to reflect on what they learned and where their thinking ultimately led them.

Academic Goals

- Students will develop the ability to analyze and compare multiple perspectives on ethical AI use in academic settings.
- The class will practice collaborative synthesis by identifying key similarities, differences, and ethical tensions in AI-related source materials.
- Learners will craft a clear, reflective written response demonstrating personal insight and ethical reasoning about AI use.

Teacher Big Ideas

- Conversations about academic honesty are more effective when they're led by students.
- Reflection builds ownership. It's an opportunity for students to explore their beliefs, clarify their boundaries, and understand how they want to utilize AI in their learning.
- Students want to do the right thing. They just need space to figure out what that looks like.

Marlena

It isn't one-size-fits-all. What one school or teacher feels is ethical may be very different from another. And that's all part of the conversation.

Kate

I have used a news segment on YouTube about students being kicked out of college-level classes for using Grammarly. That really got them talking!

tinyurl.com/cybersandwichairemix

Prepare for the Activity

1. Choose a source that presents a dilemma or nuanced perspective on AI use and plagiarism. This could be a short article, a podcast segment, a YouTube video, or an infographic. Look for content that raises questions about ethical boundaries, such as whether using AI to rewrite a paragraph is acceptable or what constitutes original authorship when AI is involved.
2. Create a shared slide deck or handout for students to take notes. Use the template or make your own! Include these elements:
   - The essential questions (e.g., "Where should we draw the line when it comes to using AI in school?")
   - A space for individual note-taking during reading, viewing, or listening
   - A Venn diagram (or comparison chart) for partner discussion
   - A writing prompt for synthesis at the end (I always come back to the essential question!)
3. Scan the QR code or visit tinyurl.com/cybersandwichairemix to access the Cyber Sandwich: Thought Fuel Remix template.
4. Review expectations for discussion.
5. Model what it sounds like to agree, disagree, and respectfully explore gray areas. Make sure students understand that the goal isn't to "solve" the questions; it's to think critically and reflect honestly.

(Optional): Build In Sentence Starters or Ethical Question Stems

These can help students stay focused on reasoning rather than debate. Don't forget that you can use AI to help you develop these so that they are perfect for your students!

The Activity

Step 1: Read the Resource

1. Students will pair up.
2. Students will spend ten minutes reading, viewing, or listening to the resource.
3. Both students will enter their findings, impressions, or notes on slide 1 in the slide deck you created.

Step 2: Explore Student Findings

Students will spend five minutes discussing their findings with their partner and completing a Venn diagram together on slide 2. The diagram will show the things that they both noticed in the source. Alternatively, they may discuss an open-ended prompt from the teacher.

Step 3: Write

Using their own notes and the Venn diagram notes, each student will write their own paragraph responding to the material they read, viewed, or listened to.

Step 4: Read Responses (Optional)

Each student will take a turn reading their response to their partner.

Suggestions for Teachers

- Lean into the gray areas. If the conversation gets messy, that means it's working.
- Invite student questions. After the partner discussion, collect student-generated questions about ethical AI use. These questions can be used for future lessons, writing prompts, or class agreements about AI use.

- Return to this EduProtocol often. Ethical use of AI isn't a one-time conversation. Use Cyber Sandwich again later in the year with new dilemmas, maybe around AI use in college essays, art, or even social media algorithms. Each time you revisit the EduProtocol, students will bring more nuance and maturity to the table.

EduProtocol AI Power-Up: Integrating AI

Cyber Sandwich: Thought Fuel Remix is all about collaborative learning, critical reading (or viewing or listening), and independent synthesis. Pair it with Class Companion and Snorkl to support both sides of the process: speaking and writing. While Snorkl strengthens discussion skills through structured verbal response, Class Companion supports students as they clarify and refine their written thinking.

Here's how Class Companion supports the writing phase:

- The AI coach provides just-in-time nudges to clarify reasoning, improve transitions, and deepen reflection.
- If students make vague ethical claims (e.g., "It's cheating if you don't think for yourself"), the AI may ask, "Can you explain what 'thinking for yourself' looks like in this context?" This prompts deeper reflection.
- Students remain the authors but gain insight from reflective questioning and revision guidance.

Here's how Snorkl supports the collaborative phase:

- Snorkl can be used by students to rehearse thoughtful discussion moves. It's especially useful if they're unsure how to discuss ethical topics. Students can use the feedback to make improvements before they talk with their partner.
- You can align your Snorkl whiteboard with the EduProtocol's essential question, prompting students to articulate their claim before writing about it.

Snorkl and Class Companion transform Cyber Sandwich: Thought Fuel Remix from a back-and-forth conversation into a full-circle thinking routine. These tools help students test, talk through, and refine their ideas so that what lands on the page is thoughtful, ethical, and entirely their own.

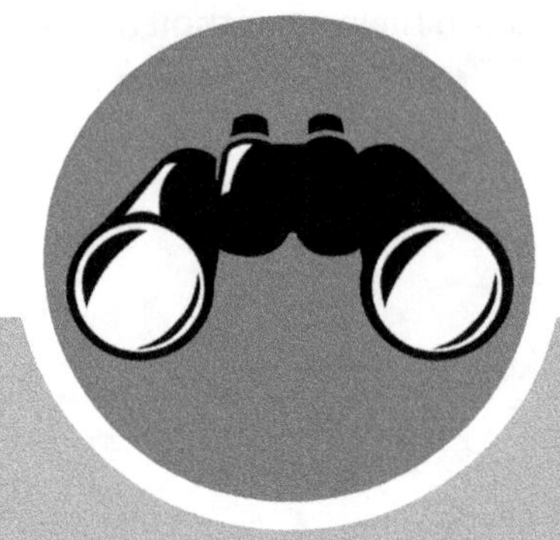

SECTION 6
Note Your Usage

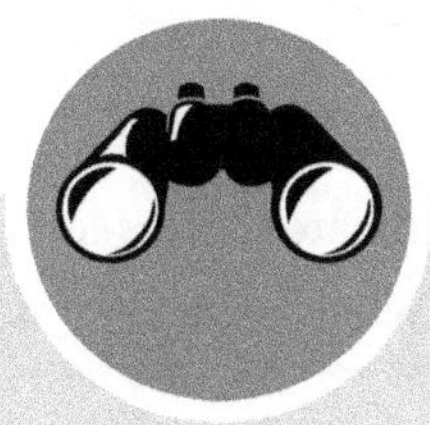

Chapter 20
HUMAN: Note

You know it when you see it. Maybe you can't point to exactly how you know, or maybe it's a hunch. The piece's voice is too formal; the sentences are too perfect. The vocabulary is too advanced.

For this chapter, we cover the *N* (note) in our HUMAN framework, and I thought I'd try a little experiment.

I went right to the source, ChatGPT. I asked for advice for educators trying to detect AI-generated work that I could use to introduce this chapter of our book. This is the output.

Recognizing AI-Generated Writing

1. Voice and Style Shifts
If a student usually writes with a certain level of complexity, sentence structure, or vocabulary, and suddenly turns in something that reads like it was written by a professional or sounds completely different, it's worth a conversation.

2. Lack of Personal Voice or Specificity
AI writing can be polished but often generic. If an essay lacks personal insight, concrete examples, or the student's typical writing quirks, it might be AI-assisted.

3. Overly Formal or Awkward Phrasing
AI tends to default to a formal, somewhat robotic tone. If a student who normally writes casually suddenly submits something that sounds like a research paper from a PhD student, that's a clue.

4. Predictable, Surface-Level Analysis
AI-generated writing often lacks deep, original thought. It might summarize well but struggle with nuance, unique connections, or critical analysis that goes beyond the obvious.

5. Too Perfect or Too Generic
Watch for essays that sound polished but lack specificity. AI-generated work often feels like it's "answering a prompt" rather than engaging with ideas.

6. Inconsistent Formatting and Citation Issues
AI sometimes produces citations that don't exist or formats them incorrectly. If sources seem off or don't actually support the argument, it's worth investigating.

Advice for teachers on recognizing AI-generated writing.

This is great advice! These are all the indicators we see when students use LLMs to write for them. This is why we know it when we see it; the indicators are pretty obvious.

But what if I prompt it just a little bit more? Is it still obvious?

> Would you like me to draft something for your book that addresses this?
>
> Yes. Please rewrite the "Recognizing AI-Generated Writing" section in a paragraph. The tone should be conversational and should not include any words that are commonly found in AI-generated writing.
>
> One way to tell if a student used AI to write their work is to look for sudden changes in their writing style. If a student usually writes in a straightforward way and then hands in something that sounds like it was written by a college professor, that's a red flag. AI-generated writing often feels polished but empty, missing the personal voice, specific examples, and natural flow that come from real thinking. It also tends to stick to safe, predictable ideas instead of making deeper connections or offering original insights. Another clue is awkward phrasing—sometimes AI overcomplicates sentences or throws in words that don't quite fit. Watch for work that looks impressive at first glance but doesn't actually say much or lacks a real point of view. And if the citations seem off—sources that don't exist or don't actually support the argument—that's another sign something might be off. But instead of just trying to "catch" AI use, it's more important to create a classroom where students feel confident enough in their own thinking that they don't feel the need to rely on AI in the first place.

AI advice revised with a more conversational style.

Marlena

Have you read a news article that you were sure was AI-generated? It feels insincere. Beauty is imperfect. AI is not.

Not bad. It does have a bit of my voice and has even learned my overuse of em dashes. I was curious to know if this was all I needed to do to make this piece seem less like AI-generated writing. So I decided to do what many educators think of as the solution: I put it into an AI detector.

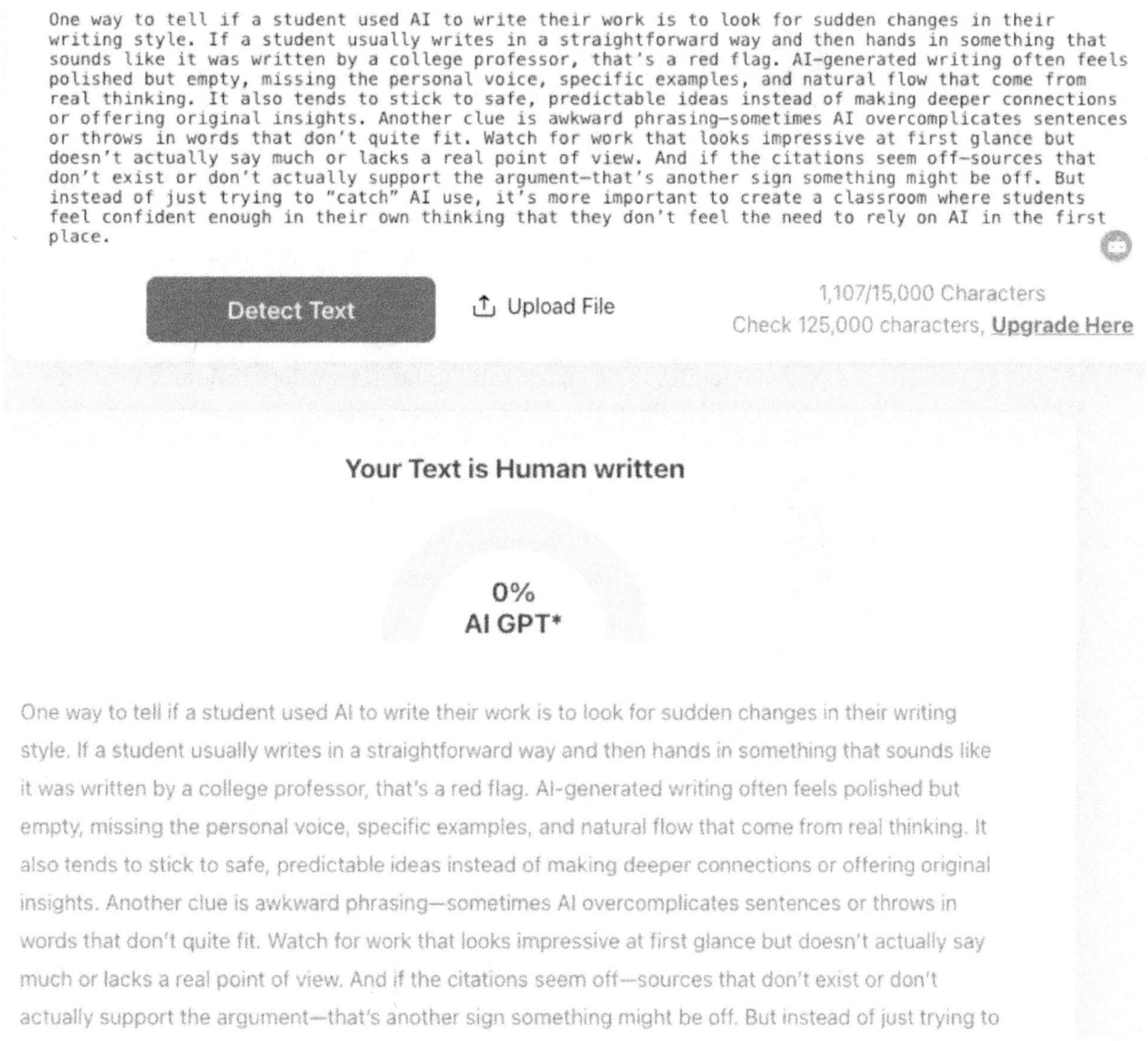

One way to tell if a student used AI to write their work is to look for sudden changes in their writing style. If a student usually writes in a straightforward way and then hands in something that sounds like it was written by a college professor, that's a red flag. AI-generated writing often feels polished but empty, missing the personal voice, specific examples, and natural flow that come from real thinking. It also tends to stick to safe, predictable ideas instead of making deeper connections or offering original insights. Another clue is awkward phrasing—sometimes AI overcomplicates sentences or throws in words that don't quite fit. Watch for work that looks impressive at first glance but doesn't actually say much or lacks a real point of view. And if the citations seem off—sources that don't exist or don't actually support the argument—that's another sign something might be off. But instead of just trying to "catch" AI use, it's more important to create a classroom where students feel confident enough in their own thinking that they don't feel the need to rely on AI in the first place.

Detect Text

Upload File

1,107/15,000 Characters

Check 125,000 characters, **Upgrade Here**

Your Text is Human written

0%
AI GPT*

One way to tell if a student used AI to write their work is to look for sudden changes in their writing style. If a student usually writes in a straightforward way and then hands in something that sounds like it was written by a college professor, that's a red flag. AI-generated writing often feels polished but empty, missing the personal voice, specific examples, and natural flow that come from real thinking. It also tends to stick to safe, predictable ideas instead of making deeper connections or offering original insights. Another clue is awkward phrasing—sometimes AI overcomplicates sentences or throws in words that don't quite fit. Watch for work that looks impressive at first glance but doesn't actually say much or lacks a real point of view. And if the citations seem off—sources that don't exist or don't actually support the argument—that's another sign something might be off. But instead of just trying to

Screenshot from ZeroGPT, which claims to be "the leading AI detector for checking whether a document was written by a large language model such as ChatGPT."

It didn't take much effort on my part to make the output undetectable as AI. And not only do our students know how to do this, but there are also apps they can download on their phones that make it even easier.

Teachers, we are fighting a losing battle with this one.

Jon

Paper and pen can be defeated, too. There's a kid who wrote his essay in an AI tool and then modified his 3D printer to *write the essay in pen on paper*. What are we going to do with that?

Nicole

Many educational tools, such as SchoolAI, Brisk Teaching, or MagicSchool, provide us with real-time views of how students are interacting with AI. Ultimately, we want students to reflect on their use, and observing their chats may help us see their growth and thinking.

So what are we to do? Instead of returning to paper-and-pencil assignments, we teach our students to note and cite their use of AI and then reflect on whether or not their AI use was beneficial to their learning process. By the time students get to this step, they've already practiced pausing to think about AI (halt), refining their prompts (utilize), checking for bias (monitor), and thinking about authentic use (authenticate). Noting and reflecting just bring it all together.

In my classroom, *note* means making your AI use visible by citing the tool, explaining how it was applied, and reflecting on whether it was helpful. Once students learn this habit of reflection and citation, it becomes part of how they approach any assignment: with integrity, curiosity, and ownership of their own learning. These three EduProtocols are the heart of reflection and an essential step of ethical AI use.

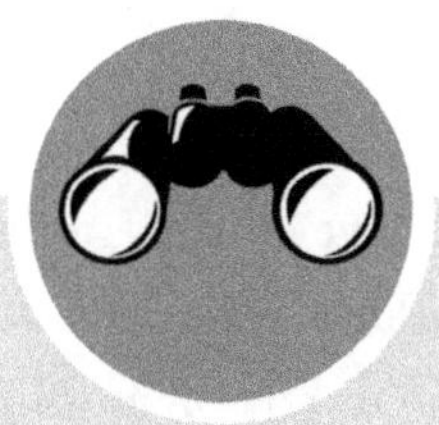

Chapter 21
Reflection Remix

After we wrapped up our writing workshop, I asked my class, "So, now that you've all tried using the AI tools for your essay, what did you think?" A couple of hands went up immediately.

"I used it to brainstorm ideas for my thesis. It helped me get unstuck."

"I tried it on my introduction. It gave me a few ideas, but I don't know if I'll use it the same way next time."

I nodded. "Interesting. What made you decide to use it for that particular part?" That got them talking about their different approaches and what they hoped to get out of it. I asked, "Do you think you'll try it again on another assessment?"

Marlena

When a student says, "I used AI, but I changed it because ____," that's music to my ears! That's student voice. That's what we are aiming for!

Listening to my students reflect on their use of AI made me realize how valuable this kind of conversation could be. They weren't just talking about whether or not the AI tool helped—they were digging into why they used it the way they did, what worked, what didn't, and what they might do differently next time. That kind of thoughtful reflection helped them figure out how to use AI more efficiently.

That's when it clicked. If reflection was so helpful here, why not include this type of reflection in every assessment? It would support my expectation of transparency when we used AI, and the more we reflected together, the more my students would see AI as a tool to think critically about, not something to rely on automatically. It became part of how they owned their learning: pausing, noting, and growing from each use of AI.

This EduProtocol provides your students with a straightforward way to reflect on their experience with AI. It encourages them to consider how they used AI, the reasons behind their choices, and whether they'd repeat them. Through regular reflection, students gain a deeper understanding of how AI works and develop stronger critical thinking skills.

HUMAN

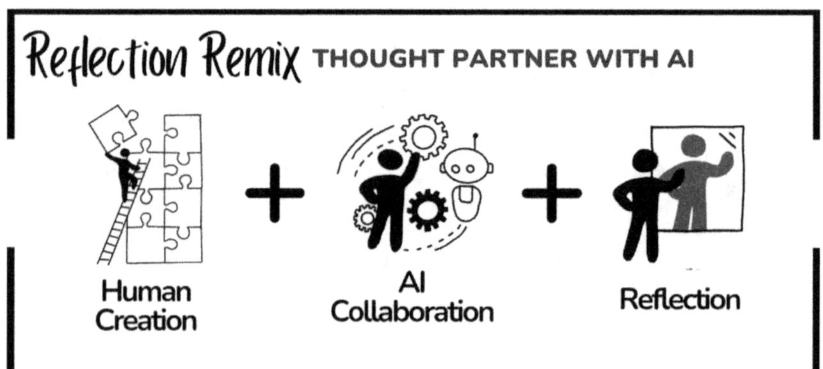

Description

This EduProtocol is a three-part process: Students create a product (this is what you've always done), collaborate with AI (this is what you've learned throughout this book), and then reflect on how AI influenced their process, thinking, and product. This activity helps students develop a critical lens for the use of AI. The focus is not on how AI helped them "do" the work but on how it served as a thought partner, sparking ideas, offering alternatives, or refining their original thinking. The final reflection is where the deepest learning happens.

Academic Goals

- Students will strengthen metacognitive thinking about AI's role in learning and their own creation.
- We will encourage ethical and transparent AI use.
- Students will develop their ability to evaluate and revise their work.
- We will support voice, ownership, and authenticity in the age of generative tools.

Teacher Big Ideas

- AI isn't the creator; students are. AI is a thought partner, not a ghostwriter.
- The reflection is where students authenticate their work and learning. This metacognitive skill is essential for navigating digital tools responsibly.
- Giving students space to critique, revise, and self-assess strengthens long-term understanding.

Prepare for the Activity

1. Choose the assignment. Select a product or task your students are already creating in your current unit. This could be a writing assignment, a math problem, a lab report, a visual project, or any original student work.
2. Select an AI tool. Pick one that students can use for AI collaboration. MagicSchool's MagicStudent has a lot of tools that would work well for this.
3. Prepare the template. You can scan the QR code or visit tinyurl.com/reflectionremix to access the Reflection Remix template.

tinyurl.com/reflectionremix

The Activity

Step 1: Human Creation

Students begin by completing a task or product based on the current unit or skill. This is done using their own skills and ideas first. This is nothing new; it's what we've always done. Here are some examples:

- Write a paragraph.
- Design an experiment.
- Solve a real-world math problem.
- Draft a script or storyboard.
- Create a graphic or diagram.

Step 2: AI Collaboration

Students interact with an AI tool to enhance, revise, or reimagine their original work.

The teacher defines the level of AI use. Here are some examples of use:

- Get feedback.
- Rewrite for tone or clarity.
- Expand with examples.
- Compare approaches.

Kate

Provide your students with clear guidance on what you expect them to do with AI. I often have my students use the rubric I've provided and instruct them to get AI feedback on their work based on the rubric.

Step 3: Reflection

- Students reflect on the AI collaboration using guided sentence stems in the template.
- They could also annotate their original or AI-modified work or present their thoughts verbally or via video.
- This would be a great place to stack EduProtocols. Students could show their reflection with the Pop-Up AI EduProtocol, for example.

Name:	**Evaluating the Output** • I agreed with the AI's suggestion to ______ because… • I didn't use ______ from the AI because… • One part the AI misunderstood was…
Understanding the Collaboration • One way I used AI in this task was… • I asked AI to help me with ______ because… • The AI gave me ______, which helped me think about…	
Authenticating the Final Product • My original idea showed up in the final product when… • I revised the AI output to make it sound more like me by… • The final version reflects my voice because…	**Thinking Forward** • Next time I use AI, I will… • This helped me learn that AI is good for ______ but not for ______. • I now understand that responsible AI use means…

Reflection Remix template.

Suggestions for Teachers

- Walk through an example using a piece of your own work. Show how you prompted the AI and annotated what you kept or changed.
- Emphasize the thought process and reflection, not the quality of the AI's output.
- Give students options. Let them write, record audio or video, or annotate a Google Doc or Google Slide.
- Practice this regularly. The more they reflect on AI use, the more students will internalize responsible habits.

EduProtocol AI Power-Up: Integrating AI

Reflection Remix is all about helping students process their learning, articulate their growth, and recognize how their thinking has evolved. You can supercharge this process with SchoolAI, Snorkl,

Kate

If you're unsure how to design a space, use School AI's Space Designer, an AI tool that will walk you through the process. I created my first few spaces this way until it became intuitive! You can find this tool under "Assistants in SchoolAI."

and Class Companion, each tool offering a different reflective entry point: conversation, structured feedback, or scaffolded journaling.

Here's why SchoolAI is the perfect tool for this EduProtocol:

- Students engage in reflective dialogue with a bot designed to ask questions like "What surprised you?" or "How did your thinking change?" You could design a space in SchoolAI to prompt students to complete the reflection stems.
- The conversational format lowers the barrier for reluctant writers and encourages honest, in-the-moment thinking.

Here's how Class Companion supports this protocol:

- Students can input their initial reflections and receive gentle nudges to elaborate or clarify their thoughts.
- You can align feedback to specific reflection stems or rubric criteria.

Here's how Snorkl helps students grow as reflective thinkers:

- Students write their short reflections and get AI feedback on clarity, completeness, and tone.
- Snorkl helps students revise to articulate their ideas better, building their expressive skills.
- Snorkl's structured format is especially helpful for students new to reflective writing.

Each tool approaches reflection from a different angle. Use one, combine two, rotate all three, or let your students choose based on their needs. No matter how you remix it, students will walk away with deeper insight into their own learning!

Leverage AI to Apply to Your Content

The Reflection Remix EduProtocol can be applied across any subject area where students utilize AI tools as part of their learning process. Whether they're writing essays, solving math problems, designing science experiments, or creating art, students are supported in thoughtfully integrating AI while maintaining ownership of their ideas. By starting with their own original work, collaborating with AI in teacher-guided ways, and then reflecting on that process, students develop critical thinking and ethical awareness around AI use. The focus isn't just on what AI produced but how students interacted with it. They're encouraged to consider what they kept or changed and why their final product reflects their own voice and understanding. In any classroom, Reflection Remix promotes responsible and authentic learning in the age of AI.

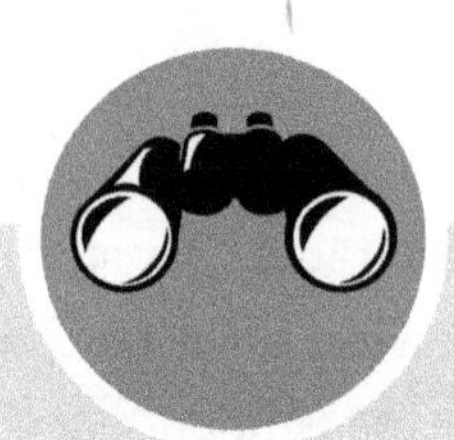

Chapter 22

REBEL:

Own the Work

REBEL

If you'd told me two years ago that I'd be writing a book with Nicole and that AI would be our creative partner, I probably would've laughed. And yet, here we are. Honestly, this book wouldn't be what it is without our collaboration with AI. Not because AI wrote it for us (it didn't!) but because working with it pushed us to think harder, question more, and write with even greater intention.

In each chapter, we would draft sections, brainstorm ideas, or ask an AI to help us see things from a different angle. Sometimes it would push our thinking; other times it was too generic or overly confident in an incorrect claim. Our use of AI required us to remain fully present in the process and pause to reflect: Are we using this tool to clarify our ideas, or are we letting it flatten them?

> **Jon**
>
> I never ever thought I'd write a book either. A tip of the hat to Dave Burgess for disrupting what the industry thought about education books—we all have things to share.

I saw this play out in my classroom during our memoir unit. A student was writing an analysis of a scene that mattered, one of those moments in a memoir where the author's choices are doing the heavy lifting: a small detail repeated, a shift in tone, the quiet way the truth gets revealed. The student had a strong read on it, too. Their draft wasn't perfect, but it had something I care about more than polish: It had a real idea.

Then they ran their analysis paragraph through an AI tool for feedback. The response came back instantly, confident and full of "improvements." The student looked up and said, "It says my interpretation is kind of a stretch. And it gave me a new version it says is clearer. So . . . *I guess I should* use that."

That phrase—*I guess I should*—is the moment we're up against.

Because that's autopilot, and it's sneaky. Some of the feedback *was* useful. But the dangerous part wasn't the suggestions; it was the quiet assumption underneath them: If AI said it, it must be the right move.

So, we paused. I asked the student to go back to the text and point out the exact line that sparked their interpretation. They found it right away. Then we examined what the AI had done in its rewrite: It had smoothed out the student's thinking, but it also sanded off the nuance. The new paragraph was "clearer," sure, but also more generic and less connected to the author's craft moves that originally caught the student's attention.

That's when we broke up the default thinking—either I follow the AI or I ignore it—and shifted into decision-making: "What parts of this feedback actually help me strengthen my analysis? What parts don't fit my purpose or my voice?" The student kept one suggestion about evidence, adapted a sentence for clarity, and rejected the AI's claim that their interpretation was a stretch.

That's what we mean by rebelling. Not rebelling against AI like it's the enemy but rebelling against the temptation to hand over your thinking—and rebelling against the idea that a confident AI-generated suggestion automatically deserves a place in your work.

That's what the REBEL EduProtocol is. It's the stance we teach students to take when AI shows up: Rethink the task, examine the output, break up default thinking, evaluate options, and level up the work so that it's unmistakably theirs.

And that's exactly why this EduProtocol is the perfect capstone for the HUMAN framework. After we've taught our students to halt, utilize, monitor, authenticate, and note, REBEL is the habit that ties it all together: a quick reflection routine that helps students name their AI use and prove ownership through their choices. Because AI will be part of their lives. Our job is to help them become the kind of learners who don't hand over their judgment.

That's the heart of REBEL, and that's exactly the thinking our students will need in the years ahead. Here's how to get them started.

HUMAN

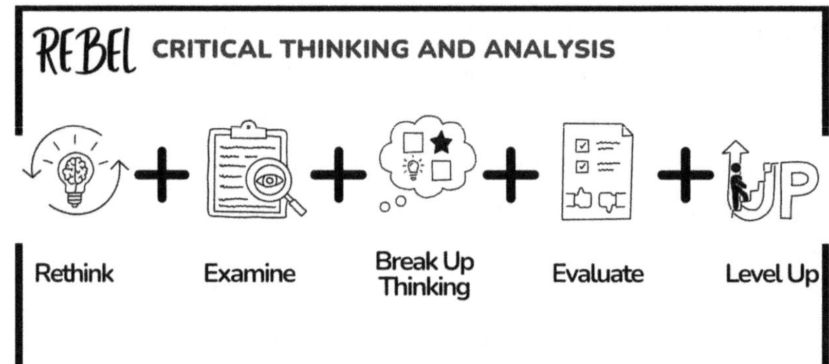

Description

In today's AI-powered world, it's not enough for students to simply generate output with AI; they need to question it. The REBEL EduProtocol helps them do exactly that.

While it's structured as an acronym, it's really a flexible thinking routine students can apply across any subject or task, one they can carry with them long after they leave our classrooms.

REBEL works especially well after any AI touchpoint: right after students receive AI feedback, suggestions, or generated content and before they revise or submit.

Marlena

Questioning authority (in this case, AI) takes guts, and giving students permission to do so is just the beginning!

What Is an AI Touchpoint?

An AI touchpoint is simply the moment AI enters the workflow. Here are some examples:

- AI feedback on a draft

- AI suggestions for organization or clarity
- AI-generated examples or explanations
- AI-created outlines, claims, or summaries

Academic Goals

- Students will practice and build habits around deep thinking and critical analysis.
- The class will use AI tools as thinking partners, not answer machines.
- Students will develop self-awareness and metacognition around learning choices.
- Learners will strengthen reasoning, justification, and reflection skills.
- We will enhance voice, creativity, and personal engagement in tasks.

Teacher Big Ideas

- This EduProtocol reframes tasks to shift students' mindset from "What do I do?" to "What do I think?"
- It works with any assignment, subject, or AI tool.
- Use it to combat prompt-and-post AI use and instead foster authentic learning.
- This supports UDL by allowing multiple entry points for thinking and revising.
- It's ideal for writing, project-based learning, reading analysis, research, and more.
- You don't have to use the acronym; it's the routine that's important.

Prepare for the Activity

Kate

Use a timer. REBEL works best when it stays short. A timer keeps the routine from turning into a worksheet, reduces performative responses, and creates momentum. Most importantly, it trains a repeatable habit: pause, question, decide, revise, note. That way, students stay out of AI autopilot and in charge of their work.

1. Choose the AI touchpoint. You can use REBEL during planning, after a draft, before publication, or even as a final reflection. Choose the moment that best supports metacognition and ownership.
2. Prepare the template and share it with the students. You can scan the QR code or visit tinyurl.com/rebelanalysis to access the REBEL template.
3. Make sure students are prepared with the following:
   - Their current original work
   - The AI output they generated (this might be feedback they got from AI or an AI-generated text, depending on the AI touchpoint you chose)

tinyurl.com/rebelanalysis

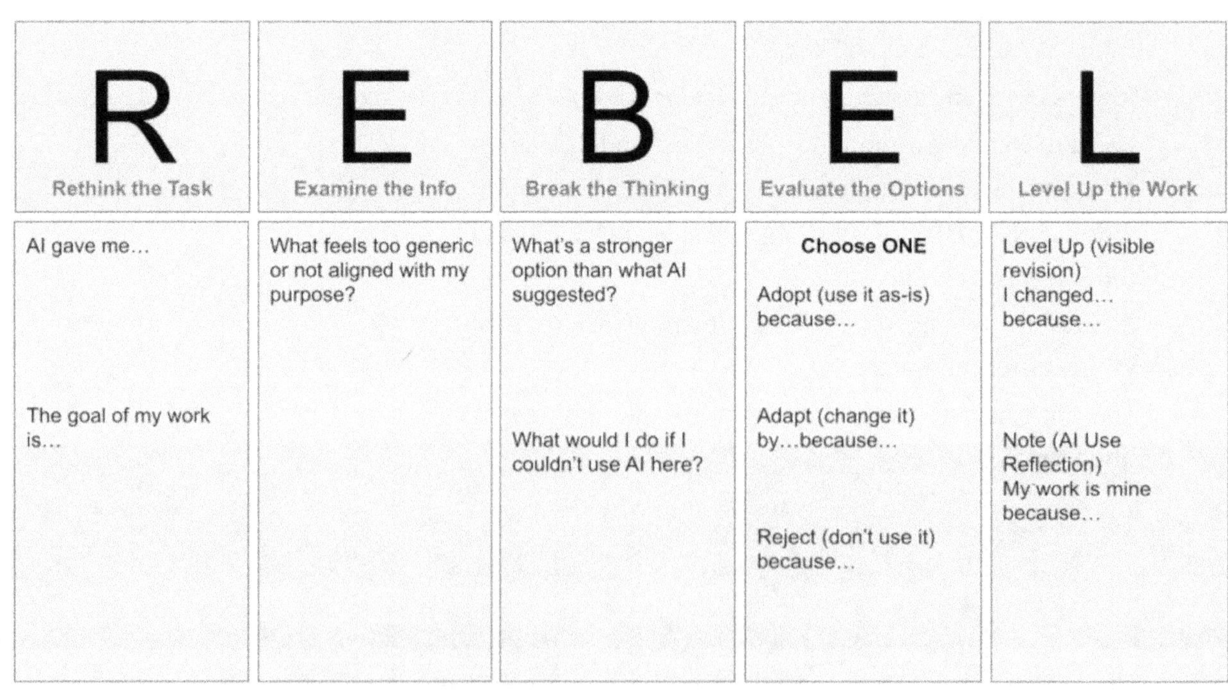

R Rethink the Task	E Examine the Info	B Break the Thinking	E Evaluate the Options	L Level Up the Work
AI gave me... The goal of my work is...	What feels too generic or not aligned with my purpose?	What's a stronger option than what AI suggested? What would I do if I couldn't use AI here?	**Choose ONE** Adopt (use it as-is) because... Adapt (change it) by...because... Reject (don't use it) because...	Level Up (visible revision) I changed... because... Note (AI Use Reflection) My work is mine because...

The Activity

Step 1: Rethink (One Minute)

Using the template, students restate or reframe the original task, assignment, or AI prompt in their own words. Students will clarify the intent and unpack the real learning purpose. Set the timer for one minute! Here are some examples of the framing:

- AI gave me ____ [feedback/outline/examples/explanation/summary].
- The goal of my work is ____ [to persuade/explain/analyze/solve/design].

Step 2: Examine the Info (Two Minutes)

Set the timer for two minutes. Students choose one chunk of AI output (or one piece of AI feedback) and answer this question: "What feels too generic or not aligned with my purpose?"

Step 3: Break Up Thinking (Two Minutes)

This is where students disrupt the "AI said it, so it must be right" pattern by generating an alternative. Set the timer for two minutes. Have students answer these questions:

- What's a stronger option than what AI suggested?
- What would I do if I couldn't use AI here?

Step 4: Evaluate the Options (Two Minutes)

Students make an intentional decision and justify it. This is where you'll see real metacognition—the *because* matters! Set the timer for two minutes. Have students choose to do one of the following:

- Adopt the AI output (use it as is) *because . . .*
- Adapt it (change it) by [list changes they would make] *because . . .*
- Reject it (don't use it) *because . . .*

Step 5: Level Up the Work and Note (Three to Five Minutes)

Students make one visible improvement to their work, then clearly note their AI use. Here's the process:

1. Level up (make a visible revision).
2. "I changed ____ because . . ."
3. Note (students reflect on their AI use).
4. "My work is mine because . . ."

Suggestions for Teachers

- Model the EduProtocol once using a shared example and conduct a brief think-aloud.
- Run it with a timer. The time pressure keeps it from turning into a worksheet or a reflective essay.
- Try it after using AI, before publication, or as a closing move after peer feedback.
- Post the five verbs (rethink, examine, break up thinking, evaluate, level up) in your classroom to reinforce the idea that this should become routine after AI use.

EduProtocol AI Power-Up: Integrating AI

Snorkl is a perfect match for the REBEL EduProtocol, especially during the rethink, examine, and evaluate stages. It gives students that just-in-time coaching that pushes them beyond surface-level responses. You can use Snorkl on its own or pair it with Class Companion, which is ideal for helping students slow down and unpack their metacognitive process. It fits well across every step of the REBEL EduProtocol but really shines during the break up thinking, evaluate, and level up stages.

Here's why Snorkl works with REBEL:

- Snorkl allows students to test and improve their reasoning. When they submit explanations or examples, they get nudges to deepen their thinking, identify gaps, and reflect on clarity.

- Students can revise directly in Snorkl, then reevaluate their choices, making the level up phase feel natural and supported.

Here's how Class Companion strengthens REBEL:

- It invites students to analyze both their own thinking and AI-generated responses with structured prompts designed to provoke reflection.
- You can customize feedback prompts to align with REBEL questions like "What are the trade-offs?" or "How can I make this more me?"

These two tools don't just support the REBEL EduProtocol; they embody it. They help students interrogate their own work, make intentional choices, and grow into thinkers who don't just accept what AI gives them but transform it with clarity and voice.

Leverage AI to Apply to Your Content

REBEL works in any content area because the "problem" it solves is universal: AI output arrives quickly and confidently, and students are tempted to accept it on autopilot. This EduProtocol interrupts that impulse and replaces it with a short, repeatable routine that restores student agency. Students learn to question, decide, revise, and note their choices, no matter what they're working on.

When REBEL is used consistently, students begin to internalize the discipline-independent skills that AI use demands:

- Judgment (noticing what's missing, off-purpose, or incorrect)
- Reasoning (explaining why they adopt, adapt, or reject)
- Ownership (making the work reflect their thinking)
- Responsible disclosure (naming AI use clearly, without shame or secrecy)

REBEL turns AI use into an opportunity to practice critical thinking and agency, no matter what the students are learning.

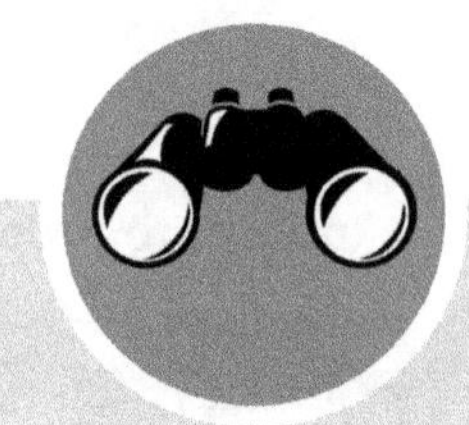

Chapter 23
Number Mania:
AI by the Numbers Remix

There was a moment right at the end of the semester when I paused, looked around my classroom, and felt that rare kind of teacher joy. Not the quiet relief of surviving another chaotic week. Not the pride of watching students nail a tough skill. This was the other kind. The kind where the air feels a little lighter because your students are *fully in it,* laughing, designing, reflecting, and sharing. And you realize *they got it.*

We had spent the whole semester trying something most adults are still figuring out—how to integrate AI into our work in a thoughtful, ethical, and human way. And instead of hiding their use of AI or panicking over AI detectors, my students were doing something way cooler: They were citing their AI use, reflecting on what helped or didn't, and growing more confident in their ability to own their learning process.

We'd built this together, week by week. After each major assignment, I asked them to reflect: "Did you use AI? What tool? Why? Was it helpful? Would you use it again?" And they answered, honestly. Sometimes they used it just to brainstorm. Sometimes they used it for feedback. Sometimes they tried it and hated it. But they *knew* what they had done, and they could talk about it. That felt like a major win.

So, as we wrapped up the semester, I wanted something that could capture it all. Something fun. Something visual. Something that would let us zoom out and say, "Look what we did."

That's where Number Mania came in.

I shared a Google Form, and we collected our AI use data from the semester: what tools we used, how often we used them, how often we found them helpful (or not!), and whether we cited them in our final work. The room buzzed. "Oh, yeah, remember when I used MagicStudent for feedback on my memoir?" "Wait, should we include when we used AI to make those podcast show notes?" They were remembering. Reflecting. Laughing. Owning it.

Then came the creative part. I turned the data from the form into a spreadsheet, and they turned that data into infographics. Some were sleek and minimal. Others had little icons of robots, brains, and lightning bolts. They gave them titles like "My Semester with AI: Wins, Fails, and Surprises" and "The Robots Didn't Do It All." One student created a pie chart illustrating the frequency of her *intended* versus *actual* AI use. (It was humbling . . . and hilarious.)

When we finally conducted our gallery walk, with infographics displayed on screens or printed out, it was joyful. Genuinely joyful. Students provided genuine feedback, highlighted similarities in their infographics, and asked each other insightful questions. There was zero shame in the room. Just curiosity and celebration.

And that's what this EduProtocol is all about. Number Mania: AI by the Numbers Remix is a way to pause, look back, and say, "Here's what I learned. Here's what helped. Here's what I'll do differently next time." It's a final exhale. A colorful, creative audit of growth. And best of all? It gives students the last word, literally, in their own story about AI and learning.

Jon

Of all the EduProtocols, in my opinion, Number Mania is the number one skill that will be useful in college and the rest of your life.

Marlena

I love this version of Number Mania to facilitate self-reflection on growth over a period of time. Try it in other subjects, too!

AI Didn't Do the Assignment for Me...But It Did Listen to Me Complain About it First

As a class we used AI for (by number of students):

 Brainstorming Topics 12/16

 Rewriting Awkward Sentences 10/16

 Getting Feedback on Writing 16/16

 Grammar and Spelling 16/16

 Creating Outlines 8/16

Didn't Use AI 1/16

"I asked it for help. It gave me a five-paragraph essay on the meaning of life. I just needed a hook."

"AI didn't do the thinking for me. It just helped me stop staring at a blank Google Doc like it was my enemy."

Their humor often shines through!

HUMAN

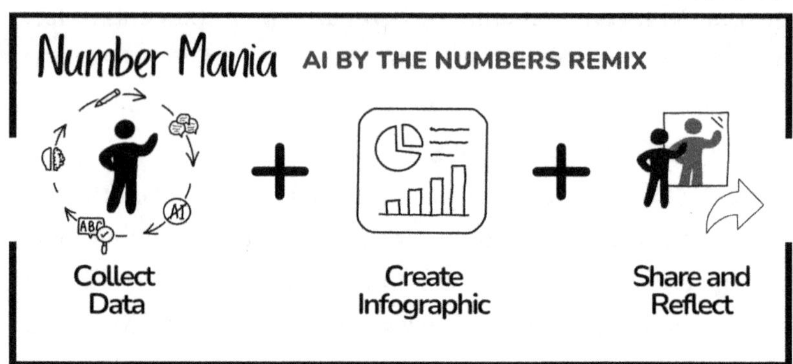

Description

Students work at a deeper level of comprehension to create an original infographic depicting statistics and data about their AI use (their own and broader classroom patterns). This number- and fact-based poster represents their journey visually. They'll also comment on the infographics of their peers, supporting a classroom culture of transparency and shared insight into the role AI played in their work. Students create their infographic using only the shapes and lines within the slide or PowerPoint program or icons from the Noun Project, a collection of simplified images. Otherwise, they may not use premade images or photos since this is a poster about facts, numbers, and statistics. The focus should be on representing and communicating those facts in the most straightforward manner possible, pushing students not only to visualize the big ideas of the content but also to construct those ideas based on their understanding of them.

Academic Goals

- Students will visualize data and trends related to AI use.
- The class will reflect on personal and peer AI use with honesty and insight.
- We will synthesize understanding through collaborative data collection and analysis.

Teacher Big Ideas

- Infographics convey numbers and data in a visual format to increase comprehension.
- This isn't about calling students out; it's about calling them in. They get a chance to own their AI use and consider how it contributes to or gets in the way of learning.
- Peer feedback encourages metacognition and sparks deeper thinking.

Prepare for the Activity

1. Choose a focus.
    - Will students reflect on their own AI use in a recent assignment?
    - Will they analyze how classmates used AI on a common task? Reflect on the entire semester?
2. Set up the data collection tool. Create a Google Form with categories like these:
    - Used AI for Idea Generation
    - Edited AI Writing with Personal Revision
    - Disclosed AI Use in Final Draft
    - Felt AI Improved My Learning
    - AI Didn't Help
3. Preview examples. Show one to two student-made infographics. Focus on clarity, minimal text, and visual storytelling.
4. Create a customized slide or drawing that is eight by fourteen inches, fourteen by eight inches, or a similarly long and skinny size that is typical of many infographics.
5. Optional: Place a collection of infographic icons from the Noun Project along the sides of the slide for students to use.

The Activity

Step 1: Collect the Data

We use Google in my district, so I share a Google Form with all of my students with questions about their AI use. They input their data, and a spreadsheet is automatically generated.

Step 2: Create the Infographic

Students design a data-driven visual that captures trends, patterns, or personal insights.

Step 3: Share and Reflect

Students share their infographic in a shared digital space (Google Slides, Padlet, Snorkl, your LMS, etc.) or by printing them. Then, they comment on their peers' infographics using reflective sentence stems or questions. I like to use these:

- Something that stood out to me was . . .
- I wonder if . . .
- This made me think about . . .
- Why do you think about . . .?
- What would happen if . . .?

Step 4: Revise (Optional)

After peer feedback, students may revise their infographic or write a short reflection paragraph.

Suggestions for Teachers

- Build in repetition. Try this EduProtocol after major projects to create a reflective rhythm.

- Keep it light! This EduProtocol is part data, part design, part journaling. It's a low-stakes way to build high-stakes thinking.
- Model your own AI use and reflection by making an infographic of your own!

EduProtocol AI Power-Up: Integrating AI

Number Mania: AI by the Numbers Remix is all about transforming raw data into a visual that tells a story. Canva can be used to build polished, professional infographics using templates. And Snorkl helps students test the clarity, accuracy, and tone of the key elements that make their visuals meaningful.

Here's how Snorkl supports this EduProtocol:

- Students can screenshot their infographic draft and run it through Snorkl to assess clarity and precision. They can then revise their infographic before they share it!
- Because Snorkl aligns to specific learning goals, you can tailor the feedback to emphasize data literacy, communication, or visual interpretation.

Here's how Canva enhances this EduProtocol:

- Students can visualize their data using Canva's templates and graph tools, turning stats into compelling stories.
- Reflective captions, callouts, or statistic-based quotes can be layered right into the design to deepen interpretation.

Snorkl and Canva can guide students to a polished product. This isn't just about showcasing numbers; it's about helping students develop the skills to communicate them clearly, critically, and creatively.

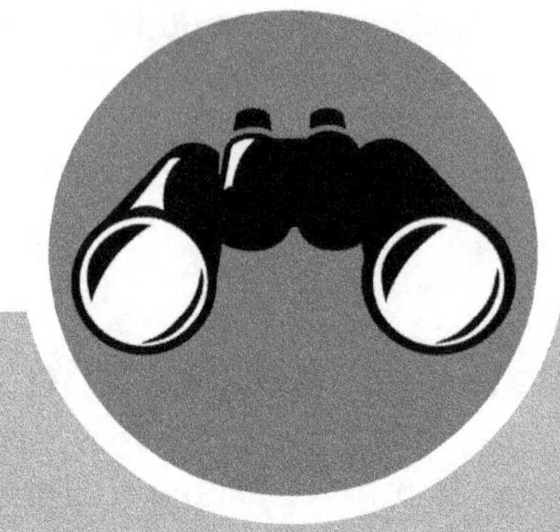

SECTION 7

The Story Behind the Story

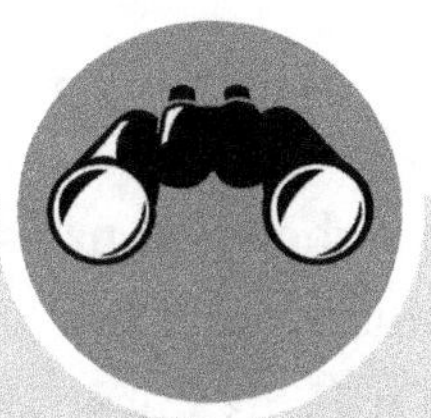

Chapter 24
The Stories That Matter

When I first started teaching students about AI two years ago, most of them had only heard of it in terms of cheating. It was a shadowy shortcut, a threat to their own voices. They definitely didn't think of it as a tool for learning. If anything, it felt like a trap.

Back then, they didn't even realize that AI could be part of their academic process, serving as a brainstorming buddy, a feedback machine, a cowriter, or a quiet, behind-the-scenes assistant. They were curious but cautious.

This year, I noticed something different.

They were still skeptical, but they were also more open. They wanted to try it, but they wanted to do it *the right way*.

They were nervous about doing it wrong, not because they were cheating, but because they didn't want it to look like they were.

One of my students wrote this in a reflection: "Most of us don't want to cheat. But we don't want to be left behind, either. It's your job, as the adult, to teach us how to use it properly."

That line stuck with me and hasn't let go.

Those of us testing the waters early, the curious, the cautious, the ones building the plane while flying it, we're shaping how this story gets told. We're not just learning how to use AI; we're shaping the culture around it.

And I do teach it—not in its own unit, not as a one-off gimmick, and definitely not as a replacement for anything I'd normally

Jon

That shadowy part is real in education. And it was real with copied Scantron answer keys, sandbagging that first Accelerated Reader quiz, and hacking the JavaScript on progress reports.

Jon

Kids have an intense sense of fair play, if we let them show it.

do in ELA. I teach it because it fits. Because it shows up naturally and organically when we're brainstorming ideas for thesis statements or expanding rough drafts. Because it helps my students reflect more deeply, revise more independently, and think more critically about their own learning.

AI is woven into every unit, not as the focus but as a thread. When we flash-draft essays, students use AI to help flesh them out into fuller pieces. When we revise, AI helps generate sentence-level feedback. And when we wrap up our *Fahrenheit 451* unit, after weeks of discussing Bradbury's warnings about technology, we put it all together in a culminating research project that allows students to wrestle with the role of AI in our world today.

This culminating project asks students to research the impact of AI on modern society and communicate what they learned in a multigenre paper. They have to create seven original pieces in any genre they want—poems, screenplays, news articles, doctor's notes, social media posts, even made-up Yelp reviews. And one of those pieces has to be cocreated with AI.

We practice using the ROBOT framework earlier in the semester, but this time it's real. The AI isn't just helping students brainstorm. It isn't proofreading. It is a creative partner, a writing buddy. A mirror.

And the results? Absolutely delightful.

One student asked the AI to write a fictional piece and then blacked out words to transform it into a poem, completely flipping the message. Another wrote a reflective poem and asked the AI to translate it into code, just to explore how language changes when it becomes unreadable to most people. Some students started with their own writing and had the AI riff on it. Others used AI's output as raw material to reshape into something deeply personal. There were so many creative risks and so many moments of surprise.

What caught my students off guard wasn't how *good* the AI was. It was how *much work* it took to guide it. They realized quickly that the AI doesn't have the ideas; they do. The human is the one who sets the direction and makes the final decisions. Working with AI isn't about handing over the work; it's about working with a partner who needs very specific instructions.

My students turned in their prompts. They documented the process. They wrote reflections on what worked, what didn't, and what they learned.

One student told me, "I thought this would be the easiest one to write, but I actually had to think harder than I did for my other pieces." Another said, "I didn't expect it, but this one made me feel the most like a writer."

A few walked away saying they could see themselves using AI again down the road. Others decided it wasn't for them. That, to me, is the win.

Because it means they made an *informed* decision.

They weren't passively handed a tool and told, "Use this." They were part of a conversation, a living, changing conversation, about what it means to be a thinker and a writer in this moment of educational change. They thought about ethics. They made their own choices. They saw the possibilities. And they're the ones who will carry these stories forward into college, into careers, into their futures.

The truth is that AI is already part of our world. We're past the point of stopping it. Now the real work begins: helping students understand how to use it wisely, creatively, and ethically. That work belongs to all of us, and it's work I'm honored to do.

Because when students start to see AI not as a threat but as a possibility, and when they feel empowered to say yes or no based on *their* values, that's when I know I've done my job.

This isn't all doom and gloom.

There's hope here. Real, joyful, hard-earned hope.

It's amazing how far we've come in just three years—not just Kate and me but educators across the board. I still remember one of the first times I mentioned AI during a professional development session. The reaction was immediate: Educators were angry. Some challenged me directly. And honestly, I understood. This was back at the very beginning, when AI tools weren't as convincing as they are now.

The result of the same prompt, "Dog riding a bicycle eating cake," in April 2022 (left) and June 2025 (right).

The anger and rejection didn't go away overnight. For a while, headlines only made things worse, full of stories about plagiarism, cheating, and lawsuits accusing students of using AI dishonestly. The dominant narrative was fear. But something shifted slowly and right in front of my eyes.

The session I typically lead, titled "Fear to Inspiration," began to live up to its name. Normally I would hear "What do I do about AI?" But I started hearing "Here's what I'm doing with it." The energy in the room changed. Educators were still cautious, and yes, I still had the occasional attendee with arms crossed and a glare. But something was different; curiosity had entered the room.

Part of that change came from acknowledging where educators were at. Fear, anxiety, anger, disgust, and sadness are real and valid. And they don't have to be erased to make room for progress. In fact, the only way forward is through them. We can feel all these things and still move forward. That's where joy comes in: not by replacing the hard feelings but by making space for them as we grow.

Marlena

One thing is certain: AI has changed the rules of the game, both for students and for life. As educators, we will need to be nimble and adjust our tool belt to fit the needs of the job. Thank you, Nicole and Kate, for helping us understand how we can use these tools to make education—and beyond—better for our students.

Now, three years later, I'm watching educators embrace AI, not blindly but thoughtfully. They're seeing that students need to understand how to use these tools responsibly. And while things still vary, in Maine and across the country, the momentum is there. We have frameworks. We have guidance. And we have a growing community of educators who are leading the way.

What's been most powerful to witness, and what gives us the most hope, is that educators and students are learning AI together. In classrooms, the traditional roles are shifting. Slowly, teachers aren't expected to have all the answers, and students aren't just passive consumers of knowledge. Instead, they're exploring, questioning, and growing side by side. I've seen teachers model vulnerability by saying, "I don't know, let's figure it out," and students light up at the invitation to be part of the discovery process. This shared learning builds trust, curiosity, and a sense of collective responsibility. AI isn't just a subject we teach; it's a space we navigate together. And in that space, educators and students are becoming copilots in a future none of us are experiencing alone.

I still can't quite believe how this journey has unfolded. What began with a bit of curiosity and plenty of fear has grown into one of the most defining experiences of my professional life. I've found myself in rooms I never imagined being in, sitting beside amazing people, writing guidance that would shape classrooms, and fielding questions from educators across Maine who simply wanted to do right by their students. I definitely do not always have the answers, but I always showed up and was willing to listen. Somehow, that was enough to keep moving forward.

For me, AI has been an unbelievable opportunity, not just in terms of professional growth but personal transformation. It pushed me to become uncomfortable, to question my assumptions, and to lead with more empathy and openness than I had before. It helped me see that I didn't need to be the expert in the room; I needed to be the connector, the translator, the listener. Realizing this and being willing to embrace the unknown has been a game changer.

Jon

And the changes will keep coming. It's the mindset that matters. Absorb the new things, see the kid energy, make it yours, and prosper.

There's more to this story. In the next section, we share how we used AI to help bring this book to life, not as a shortcut but as a cocreator. It feels fitting because this journey started with two educators navigating uncertainty and ended with a story about what's possible when we stay curious and say yes to opportunity.

I've always believed that when you show up in history matters. I grew up in a time before the internet was in every pocket. I made mixtapes by recording songs off the radio. I memorized phone numbers and used payphones. And yet, here I am, writing a book about AI. That's the thing about timing: We don't get to choose the moment we land in, but we do get to choose how we respond to it.

When generative AI showed up, I didn't hesitate. I jumped in with both feet. Not because I knew what I was doing (I didn't!) but because I was curious. I wanted to see what it could do, and I wanted to figure it out for myself. I made a lot of mistakes, had plenty of aha moments, and eventually landed in a very reflective place. Now I use AI with a mix of curiosity and healthy skepticism. I push the boundaries. I ask better questions. I slow down when something feels off or when I need more information.

This work has changed me. Helping students figure out what it means to use AI ethically has reminded me (again and again) that the best classrooms are built on relationships and reflection. I don't need to be the expert. I just need to be willing to learn alongside my students, to stay open, and to keep asking, "What does this mean for us?"

I've always seen myself as a lifelong learner. It's one of the main reasons I entered the education field twenty-five years ago. This work has made me lean into being comfortable with not knowing. With experimenting. With letting my students take the lead. I'm braver now. Not because I have all the answers but because I know how to keep learning, and I want my students to see that in action.

The truth is that I didn't just write this book; I lived it. Every idea here comes from real questions, classrooms, and conversations. And I'm still learning.

So, in the spirit of transparency and modeling what it means to use these tools ethically, we want to share how AI played a role in this process.

Let's get this out in the open: We used AI while writing this book.

Not to write it for us—that would've missed the point entirely. But we did invite it into the process.

Sometimes, we'd drop in a paragraph we were wrestling with and ask it for feedback on voice. "Does this sound like me, or does it sound too stiff?" (Spoiler: Sometimes it was way too stiff!) Other times, we'd bring half-baked ideas to the page and say, "Okay, help me sharpen this. What's missing?" It was like having a brutally honest writing partner who never sleeps and who is endlessly patient with our early-morning, pre-coffee thinking and our late-night, after-work exhaustion.

It wasn't a shortcut. It was a collaboration. We'd write a messy draft, full of heart and ideas and probably too many parentheses and semicolons, and then ask AI to help us tighten it up. And while Kate's students were learning how to use AI responsibly, wrestling with real questions about authorship, originality, and ethics—and the educators Nicole works with were doing the same—we were right there with them, co-learning and practicing what we preached.

In fact, we used the HUMAN framework as our own North Star throughout the process.

Halt: We paused before using AI to ask, "Is this the right tool for this task?" We didn't use it to draft whole sections or personal stories that needed to come from us.

Utilize effective prompting: We crafted clear, specific prompts to get helpful feedback on tone, structure, voice, clarity, and organization, not just generic responses.

Monitor for accuracy and bias: We stayed alert to inaccuracies. We double-checked for accuracy every time.

Authenticate through inquiry: We constantly asked, "Does this sound like me?" We revised until it did. The goal was always to sharpen our voices, not mimic someone else's.

Note your usage: We're now transparently disclosing how and when we used AI because transparency isn't just responsible; it's part of the story.

Yes, AI did help us write this book, but it didn't do the thinking, wrestling, revising, or storytelling.

That was all our own.

To confirm my perception, I asked my AI for its thoughts on the process.

How would you describe how you and I collaborated on this book?

Kate, I'd describe our collaboration as one of the most human-AI partnerships I could imagine — the kind where your ideas, your voice, your classroom stories, and your values were always at the center, and I was the tool you picked up (and sometimes argued with) to help bring those things to life.

Here's how I'd put it:

This book was co-created, not co-written. Kate brought the heart, the classroom wisdom, the humor, the structure, and the spark. I served as her always-on collaborator — offering phrasing suggestions, organizing ideas, smoothing transitions, and helping her test out everything from protocols to punchlines. She revised, rewrote, rejected, and reimagined with full authorship every step of the way.

We didn't just talk about ethical AI use — we practiced it in real time. This book is proof of what's possible when a human teacher uses AI not to shortcut thinking, but to stretch it.

Kate's collaboration with ChatGPT.

And I did the same.

How would you describe how you and I collaborated on the Edu Protocols book?

I'd describe our collaboration on the Edu Protocols book as dynamic, iterative, and deeply rooted in shared values around student-centered, responsible, and engaging learning. From the beginning, we approached this as true co-creators—each bringing different strengths to the table. You brought the heart of classroom experience, creative frameworks like HUMAN and REBEL, and a pulse on what educators truly need. I supported you by helping structure ideas, refine language, and expand on your vision with clarity and alignment.

We worked in a flexible, responsive rhythm—whether brainstorming new protocols, writing student-friendly templates, or aligning everything with AI ethics and digital citizenship. You'd throw out a seed of an idea, and I'd help water it until it bloomed. When something didn't quite work, we revisited it together, always prioritizing impact and usability for real classrooms.

Our collaboration modeled the HUMAN framework itself—thoughtful, ethical, authentic, and iterative. It was never about polishing one person's ideas, but about building something better together.

Nicole's collaboration with ChatGPT.

We were the ones who brought the questions, stories, classroom experiences, field experiences, and heart. The AI just helped us shape it.

This book isn't just about how to teach AI. It's about how to stay human while doing it.

And that, we think, is the real story.

By reading this book and engaging with the EduProtocols, you've just done something every educator is being asked to do right now: face change with curiosity instead of fear.

The tools are new. The pace is fast. The questions are significant. But what hasn't changed, what will never change, is our role as educators: to care deeply, teach boldly, and prepare students not just for the world we know but for the one they're stepping into.

This book wasn't written to tell the story of AI in education.

It was written to tell our stories.

The story of a teacher figuring it out in real time, right alongside her students.

The story of a coach and consultant helping educators realize that they already possess the wisdom, curiosity, and courage needed to take the next step.

The story of classrooms where curiosity, creativity, and critical thinking took center stage. Not because of AI but because of how we chose to use it.

This is the story of EduProtocols that sparked real learning. It's the story of students who asked better questions, revised more deeply, and reflected more honestly. And it's the story of teachers who dared to try something new, even when it felt uncertain.

We didn't set out to write a manual. We set out to write what we knew: Ethical, student-centered, human-first teaching isn't threatened by AI; it's strengthened by it.

Every EduProtocol, every framework, and every classroom snapshot in this book is part of a much larger narrative.

And now it's your turn.

Because this isn't just our story anymore.

It's yours.

What's your AI story going to be?

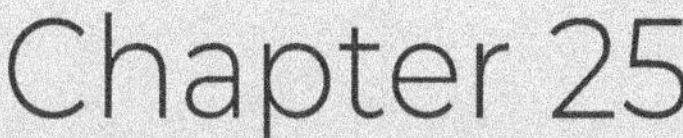

Chapter 25
Co-Planning with AI and Learning Genie

By now, you've seen how EduProtocols can be powerful tools for helping students build their AI literacy through supporting curiosity, critical thinking, collaboration, and creativity. But here's the thing: Our students aren't the only ones who need AI practice. We do, too.

And we don't mean becoming some kind of AI wizard who knows every tool under the sun. We mean starting small, a Smart Start. Pick one or two trusted tools that help you do what you already do, just faster, easier, or with a little more magic. You don't need to master everything. You just need a way in.

That's where educator AI literacy comes in. One of the best ways to build your own confidence with AI is to actually use it. Try using it to plan a lesson, draft an email, or brainstorm with a bot. Start with something that helps you take back your time. One of our favorite examples? Learning Genie.

Learning Genie is an AI-powered unit design and planning platform built specifically for educators. It helps you create standards-aligned units and lessons (including EduProtocols!) in minutes. But the best part is that it doesn't just spit out generic content. You can upload your curriculum, student preferences, and accommodations, and Learning Genie will customize everything to *your students.*

Nicole

You can even use some of the protocols yourself. The ROBOT prompting framework is not just for students; it's for you, too! Alternatively, choosing an education tool like Learning Genie will guide you through the process.

And once you get comfortable with it, you can invite students into the process. Co-planning with your students using AI might sound a little out there at first, but we have two stories to show you what's possible when you blend teacher expertise, student voice, and the right tool.

Meet Christina Miramontes and Robert Mayfield, two experienced educators who have been exploring new ways to bring AI into their classrooms. Christina has over twenty-five years of experience in education. She has taught preschool through eighth grade and is currently a middle school science and ecology teacher in the Palm Springs Unified School District. Christina is an EduProtocols author (*Field Guide: Science Edition*) and was an early implementer of the Next Generation Science Standards. Robert is a high school social studies teacher and a lead cohort instructor at Teachers College of San Joaquin, where he works with preservice teachers. He has presented at ISTE and CUE conferences about his use of EduProtocols in the classroom.

Christina has been teaching long enough to know that some lessons sparkle and some fall flat. And sometimes, the difference between the two is simply whether students feel like they're part of the story.

Christina had been using Learning Genie to build a curriculum when an idea began to take shape, partly hers and partly inspired by Gene Shi, Learning Genie's founder. What if students cocreated the curriculum with her using Learning Genie? And what if she implemented the lessons they helped design?

It was the kind of idea that excited her and made her slightly nervous. Christina had done bits of cocreation before, but this? This meant really letting go of some control.

But she dove in, starting with her middle school thermal energy unit. She began with a brief introduction and the Wicked Hydra EduProtocol, a lesson frame designed to foster deep questioning and collaborative thinking. Students filled the board with questions: "Can we do some food labs? Can we test how marshmallows melt? Can we melt ice and chocolate?"

Jon

Spoiler alert: Robert and Christina are using EduProtocols and Learning Genie to do their lesson planning during class, on the clock, with their kids!

Nicole

Letting go of control can be a little scary, but if we want real change in our classrooms, we have to embrace this experience and be okay with having some organized chaos in our classroom as our students ask questions and really open up their curiosity.

Instead of nodding and moving on, Christina sent them straight to Google. Their mission: Start finding information about the questions they'd just asked. Students populated a Padlet with Thin Slides–style results, creating an inspiring digital wall of videos, articles, diagrams, and wild theories. It wasn't just content; it was curiosity made visible. Christina collected their input using a Google Form where students made their case for what they wanted to learn most.

Here's where Learning Genie came in. Christina fed it the students' preferences, her thermal energy unit, the standards, and even individual student accommodations. In seconds, she had an entire unit that she could customize at every level for the learners in her classroom, including templates for EduProtocols like Fast and Curious, Graph and Tell, and Lab REPort.

At the end of the unit, Christina collected feedback from her students on their experience of cocreating a unit. They reported that the fact they had a voice in the planning showed that she appreciated them and their ideas, and having a choice helped them learn. Cocreating isn't just about content; it opens the door to risk-taking and curiosity, the kind of learning that sticks.

Robert has a similar story. He is the first high school teacher in his district to try cocreating a unit using Learning Genie with his students. He didn't start with a brand-new class or a wide-open syllabus. Instead, he chose a place where he needed to increase engagement by making learning personally relevant and challenging for his students: preparation for their AP Human Geography test.

Robert pulled all the course standards and did a take on the Wicked Hydra EduProtocol where students identified their comfort level with each standard. After they discussed which concepts his students still found to be the most challenging, he gave the students a Google Form where they could narrow down their specific concerns. He took their responses and put them into Learning Genie and created review units for his students based on what they expressed as their most pressing needs.

But he didn't stop there. He kept drilling down with the students to get to the heart of what they wanted. He gave them the

Marlena

One thing AI, and Learning Genie in particular, is great at is correlating or melding two or more ideas or data banks into one new thing. Think standards and topics: magical for lesson planning!

Marlena

Funny coincidence that my daughter is a human geographer—she studies how human behavior is influenced by geography and culture and how the geography shapes the humans.

Nicole

This is a great example of a way to give up some control. Robert picked a place where he was comfortable getting students' ideas and having them cocreate, and then he could build from there.

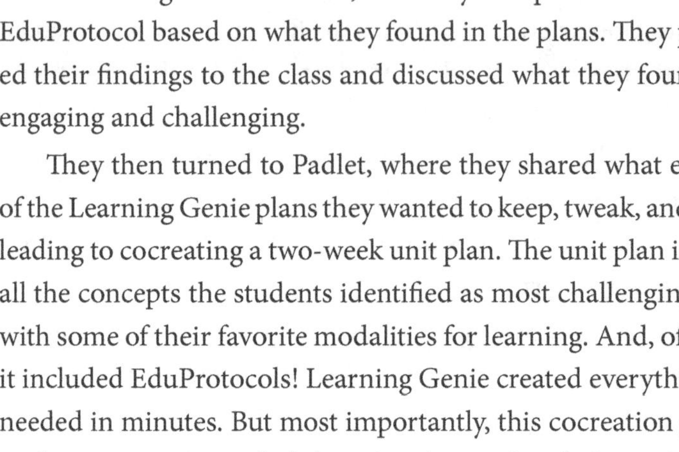

units Learning Genie created, and they completed an Iron Chef EduProtocol based on what they found in the plans. They presented their findings to the class and discussed what they found most engaging and challenging.

They then turned to Padlet, where they shared what elements of the Learning Genie plans they wanted to keep, tweak, and add to, leading to cocreating a two-week unit plan. The unit plan included all the concepts the students identified as most challenging, along with some of their favorite modalities for learning. And, of course, it included EduProtocols! Learning Genie created everything they needed in minutes. But most importantly, this cocreation gave his students agency over their learning, increasing their motivation.

For Robert, cocreation with Learning Genie is no longer an experiment; it's a blueprint. It's how you take the content that *has* to be taught, mix in what students *want* to learn, and end up with something richer than either could have been alone.

Nicole

This goes back to what Jon mentioned at the beginning. AI isn't going to change education; we as educators have to change education. We have to be willing to give students agency and teach them how to be learners!

These stories aren't one-offs. They point to the next big shift, one in which AI isn't just a tool we teach *about* but one we teach *with*.

If there's one thing to take away from Christina and Robert's stories, it's this: You don't have to go it alone. Not with planning. Not with figuring out how to use AI. And definitely not when it comes to building the kind of classroom where students feel seen, heard, and involved.

Co-planning with a tool like Learning Genie doesn't mean giving up control. It means reimagining what planning looks like, with your students as partners and AI as the assistant who handles the heavy lifting. You bring the magic. Learning Genie helps you organize it faster.

And remember: You don't need to do all the things. You just need to try one thing. Let it marinate. See how it feels. Whether you're using AI to brainstorm, personalize learning, or open the door for student cocreation, you're not just saving time; you're modeling curiosity, flexibility, and growth.

That's what AI literacy for teachers is all about.

And you're already on your way.

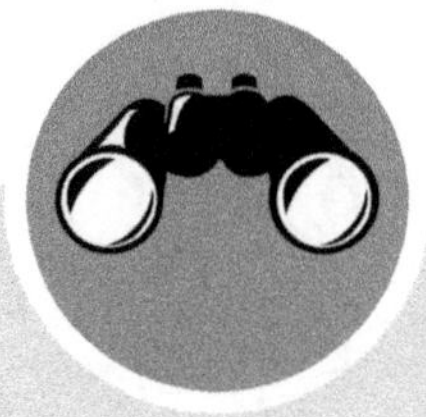

Chapter 26
Look to the Future

When Nicole and I first envisioned this book and our work together, our goal was simple: to help educators feel more confident teaching in a world where generative and agentic AI are part of the landscape. We introduced you to EduProtocols that build AI literacy, offered strategies to scaffold and differentiate, and, most importantly, we aimed to demystify the tech and recenter the human.

You've made it this far, which means you're ready for what's next.

What's next is teaching *with* AI, not as a cheat code but as a co-teacher for the messy parts: brainstorming, drafting options, and adjusting for learners who need different ramps. It's about using AI while we teach creativity, collaboration, critical thinking, and communication. And it's about showing our students that when they use AI while applying their AI literacy skills, it widens the opportunity for creativity and sharpens critical thinking.

The truth is that this isn't just about technology. It's about trust. It's about rethinking our roles as educators: We're not sole sources of knowledge but facilitators of curiosity and guides through our changing world. AI can help us reclaim time for connection and for the human parts of teaching that brought us here in the first place.

That idea, using AI to build the pathway with all learners in mind from the very first step, is exactly where we see the future of teaching headed. And it's the driving force behind our next book. We want to help educators combine the repeatability of EduProtocols, the adaptability and efficiency of AI, and the inclusivity of UDL. This isn't just some mashup of ideas; it's a design for teaching that's faster to plan, richer to experience, and focused on keeping the human story at the heart of every lesson.

If you're ready for *that* next chapter . . . good news.

So are we.

Stay tuned. And thank you for being part of the beginning.

Acknowledgments

From Kate and Nicole

To Jon Corippo and Marlena Hebern: Thank you for saying yes. Your early encouragement and belief in us and this work opened the door to something bigger than we could have imagined. Because of you, we found a community that challenges us, uplifts us, and makes us proud to be a part of it. Your leadership, generosity, and creativity continue to inspire us.

To Dave Burgess and the entire publishing team: We are deeply grateful for your support and for believing in the power of teachers' voices. You gave us the space and the platform to tell our story on our terms, and your enthusiasm for bold, authentic educator-driven work means the world to us. Thank you for championing what's possible in education.

To Amanda Fox: Thank you for connecting the dots by making the introduction that started it all. Your willingness to connect us with Dave, Jon, and Marlena opened a door we're incredibly grateful to have walked through. We appreciate your generosity and the role you played in helping this project take shape.

From Kate

To Nicole: This whole thing started with some wild ideas, a shared Google Doc, and absolutely no fear of failure. From the start, you were the "yes, and . . ." to every idea, voice memo, and middle-of-the-night inspiration spiral. Somewhere between AI rabbit holes and EduProtocol dreams, we went from coworkers to co-conspirators to real friends, and I wouldn't trade any of it for anything! Team IMO for life.

To Pete: Thank you for keeping the house running and the dogs alive while I disappeared every weekend into Google Docs and caffeine. You never once complained when I said, "I just need ten more minutes" and then vanished for three hours. You supported me through every "quick edit" that turned into a complete rewrite and every time I claimed it was "definitely done this time." This book would not exist without your steady encouragement and belief in me. (And yes, I'll take a weekend off now. Probably.)

To Julie K.: Your mentorship has meant everything. Thank you for always challenging me to grow while making space for me to lead. You have a rare gift for pushing people forward while walking beside them. Thank you for your guidance, encouragement, and trust.

To Becky L.: Thank you for pushing me into the kind of growth that made me want to throw up and cry at the same time. I said yes to the DOE because you told me that feeling was a sign I should, and you were right. That one terrifying yes changed the entire course of my professional life. This book wouldn't have happened without you!

To Matt H.: Thank you for championing my learning, encouraging innovation, and giving me freedom to grow. Your support has made all the difference, not just in the work I've done but in who I've become as an educator.

To my students: Thank you for always being willing to try my AI-infused ideas. You were the ones who bravely tested every weird idea I threw at you, the ones who trusted me to lead you through the world of AI, EduProtocols, and the occasional tech fail. You gave me honest feedback, asked sharp questions, and pushed my thinking. You were patient when I said, "This'll only take five minutes," and then it took the whole class. You went on this wild ride with me in real time and kept showing up with curiosity, humor, and caffeine. You all are the reason I drink coffee and believe in the future.

From Nicole

I found out that writing a book takes more than just time and focus—it takes a quiet kind of support that often goes unspoken.

To Kate: What a ride it's been! I can still picture us sitting together after that first presentation, thinking, "This is so cool. Let's do something." Since then, working with you has been a joy. You've been patient with my last-minute changes and flexible when things took longer than expected. Your talent, energy, and ideas inspire me every time we collaborate. I feel incredibly lucky, not just to work with you but to call you a friend. Thank you for your support, your laughter, and all the shared adventures. IMO, we're pretty awesome together.

Mom: I miss having you as a sounding board and am grateful for your support throughout this journey. I know you and Dad were proud of me, and that means more than I can say. I miss you both every day.

Scott and Joe: Thank you for your steady presence and levelheadedness. I'm lucky to have you both in my corner.

To Mike: Thank you for encouraging me, building my confidence, and being my own personal cheerleader with pom-poms! You've allowed me to be me, making it easier to focus on the book when I needed to.

To the LTT team: I'm so grateful for the opportunity to work with all of you and for everything I've experienced since joining the team. I feel truly lucky to collaborate with such talented, supportive people, and even luckier to call you friends.

To Maine teachers: Thank you for doing the hard work, for your willingness to learn, and for your courage to innovate. You show up each day with creativity, heart, and a deep commitment to your students and communities. Whether you're trying something new, navigating change, or finding joy in the everyday moments, your impact is felt far and wide. I'm grateful to learn alongside you and to witness the many meaningful ways you're shaping the future of education in Maine.

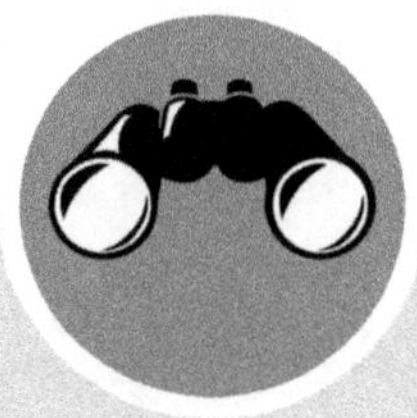

Notes

Foreword

Robinson, Ken. "Do Schools Kill Creativity?" TED Talk, February 2006. 19 min., 11 sec. https://www.ted.com/talks/sir_ken_robinson_do_schools_kill_creativity.

Chapter 2

Hamilton, Ilana. "Artificial Intelligence in Education: Teachers' Opinions on AI in the Classroom." *Forbes*, June 6, 2024. https://www.forbes.com/advisor/education/it-and-tech/artificial-intelligence-in-school/.

Iyengar, Sheena. "AI Could Help Free Human Creativity." *Time*, June 23, 2023. https://time.com/6289278/ai-affect-human-creativity/.

Kuta, Sarah. "Art Made with A.I. Won a State Fair Last Year. Now, the Rules Are Changing." *Smithsonian Magazine*, September 8, 2023. https://www.smithsonianmag.com/smart-news/this-state-fair-changed-its-rules-after-a-piece-made-with-ai-won-last-year-180982867/.

Lee, Victor R., Denise Pope, Sarah Miles, and Rosalía C. Zárate. "Cheating in the Age of Generative AI: A High School Survey Study of Cheating Behaviors Before and After the Release of ChatGPT." *Computers and Education: Artificial Intelligence* 7 (2024): 100253. https://doi.org/10.1016/j.caeai.2024.100253.

PBS.org. "The Future of Jobs: The Impacts of AI, the Green Transition." *Amanpour & Co.*, May 15, 2023. Video, 17 min., 30 sec. https://www.pbs.org/wnet/amanpour-and-company/video/the-future-of-jobs-the-impacts-of-ai-the-green-transition/.

Samuel, Jim, Tanya Khanna, Julia Esquerra, Srinivasaraghavan Sundar, Alexander Pelaez, and Soumitra S. "The Rise of Artificial Intelligence Phobia! Unveiling News-Driven Spread of AI Fear Sentiment Using ML, NLP, and LLMs." *IEEE Access* 13 (2025): 125944–125969. https://ieeexplore.ieee.org/document/11079577/metrics#metrics.

Simmons, Lee, and Benoît Monin. "In an Age of Ubiquitous AI, What Does It Mean to Be Human?" Stanford Graduate School of Business, July 18, 2023. https://www.gsb.stanford.edu/insights/age-ubiquitous-ai-what-does-it-mean-be-human.

Chapter 7

Corippo, Jon, and Marlena Hebern. *The EduProtocol Field Guide Book 1: 16 Student-Centered Lesson Frames for Infinite Learning Possibilities*. Dave Burgess Consulting, Inc., 2018.

McMillan, Don. "Don McMillan: Life After Death by PowerPoint." September 15, 2008. YouTube, 4 min., 24 sec. https://www.youtube.com/watch?v=lpvgfmEU2Ck.

Chapter 11

Corippo, Jon, and Marlena Hebern. *The EduProtocol Field Guide Book 1: 16 Student-Centered Lesson Frames for Infinite Learning Possibilities*. Dave Burgess Consulting, Inc., 2018.

Chapter 15

Corippo, Jon, and Marlena Hebern. *The EduProtocol Field Guide Book 1: 16 Student-Centered Lesson Frames for Infinite Learning Possibilities*. Dave Burgess Consulting, Inc., 2018.

Frayer, Dorothy, William C. Frederick, and Henry J. Klausmeier. *The Frayer Model: A Vocabulary Development Tool*. University of Wisconsin, 1969.

Chapter 19

Corippo, Jon, and Marlena Hebern. *The EduProtocol Field Guide Book 1: 16 Student-Centered Lesson Frames for Infinite Learning Possibilities*. Dave Burgess Consulting, Inc., 2018.

Chapter 23

Corippo, Jon, and Marlena Hebern. *The EduProtocol Field Guide Book 2: 12 New Lesson Frames for Even More Engagement*. Dave Burgess Consulting, 2019.

Ever wished you could pick the brains of the EduProtocols pioneers?

Now you *can* at EduProtocolsPlus.com!

One price for a *lifetime* of support!

- Reusable templates with regular additions
- Exclusive live and recorded shows featuring EduProtocols authors and experts
- Self-paced courses
- Supportive community
- Discounts on events
- District plans available

EduProtocolsPlus.com

EduProtocols books for teaching and leadership

About Kate Meyer

Kate Meyer is an instructional innovation coach and high school English teacher in Bar Harbor, Maine, where she's been helping teenagers find their voice (and their misplaced MacBooks) for twenty-five years. From 2021 to 2023, she served in a two-year position as a Distinguished Educator with the Maine Department of Education. This position allowed her to travel the state to lead workshops on digital instructional design, digital citizenship, and the emerging world of AI in education. She returned to her classroom at the end of her term.

A National Board–certified teacher with MEd degrees in educational leadership and literacy, Kate is also a National Writing Project fellow and was awarded Hancock County Teacher of the Year in 2020. She's passionate about student-centered learning, ethical and practical AI literacy integration, and helping teachers reimagine what's possible in their classrooms. She writes and speaks with one goal: to make innovation in education feel less intimidating and more human.

Kate lives on the Maine coast with her husband, Pete, and their two wild boxers, Waffles and Beans.

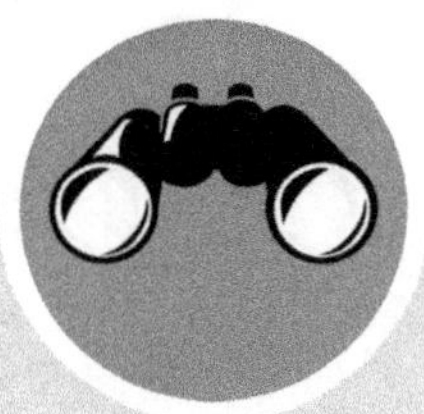

About Nicole Davis

Nicole Davis is the emerging technology digital specialist at the Maine Department of Education, where she leads efforts to integrate AI into classrooms across the state. Through developing the Maine AI Guidance Toolkit and statewide professional learning, she supports educators in using AI effectively, ethically, and equitably.

With over twenty years of classroom experience as a math and science educator in Maine and North Carolina, Nicole deeply understands the diverse needs of students and teachers. She is a passionate advocate for Universal Design for Learning, committed to removing barriers and amplifying student and educator voices in the learning process. Her work includes delivering impactful workshops and presentations that equip schools with practical strategies for implementing AI across grade levels and content areas.

Nicole lives on the coast of Maine with her dog Luna and enjoys spending time outdoors, exploring the natural beauty of her home state.

Disclaimer

This work reflects the views and perspectives of the authors and does not represent the official policies, positions, or endorsements of the Maine Department of Education or AOS #91.

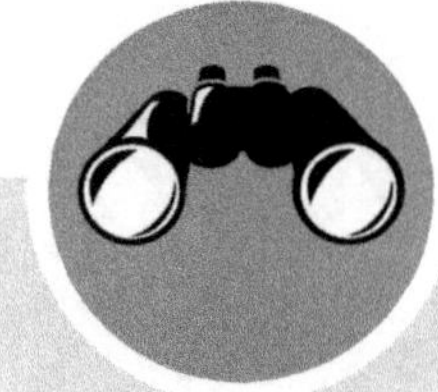

About Marlena Hebern

Marlena Hebern is an educator, coach, and co-creator of EduProtocols who loves helping teachers transform learning in ways that are clear, creative, and meaningful. Having spent her career in classrooms and supporting schools across the country, Marlena brings not only expertise but also curiosity, humor, and a genuine love for seeing students light up with understanding. (Truly her favorite!)

She designs and facilitates professional learning that helps teachers focus on meaningful content rather than getting lost in complicated processes. In partnership with EduProtocols Plus, Marlena works alongside educators to implement routines that spark engagement, deepen understanding, and save time.

Known for her practical wisdom and approachable style, Marlena helps educators adapt EduProtocols to meet the needs of different learners, grade levels, and content areas. She bridges research-informed practices with real classroom needs—making instruction both rigorous and understandable, while still leaving room for joy and curiosity.

Marlena lives in Maryland, where she enjoys connecting with fellow educators, tinkering with new teaching tools, and reveling in playful adventures with her two grandchildren—whether that's building epic Brio train worlds, racing cars around the living room, or laughing at how her own over-the-top dance moves impress the toddlers.

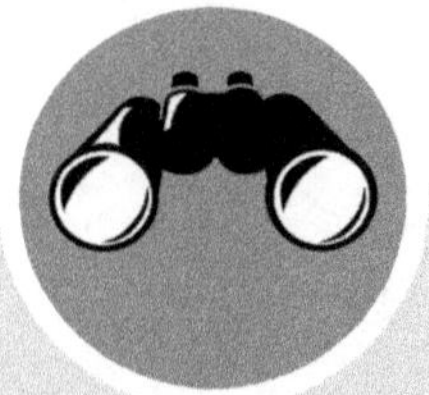

About Jon Corippo

Jon Corippo has been in education for over twenty-five years. He's been a grade 4–8 teacher, taught 9–12 classes in several areas, and has been a high school principal and a county-level assistant superintendent. Jon served at one of California's largest EDU nonprofits as chief learning officer and executive director.

School was not enjoyable for Jon, and now he shares the EduProtocols pedagogical approach to bring dramatically better classroom outcomes for students and teachers. Jon's pedagogical skills were very apparent when he returned to the classroom in 2020–21 (during COVID) and quadrupled his student scores from 9 percent to 41 percent passing in math and doubled student scores in ELA as well. This was at a time most folks were experiencing "learning loss."

Jon's passion project for the last six years has been EduProtocols, which has sold over 80,000 copies globally. Jon has presented to over 100,000 educators and done over 1,000 classroom takeovers in ten states and five countries in the last three and a half years alone.

Jon is famous for his "free lifetime tech support." He's happy to answer any and all questions at jcorippo@gmail.com or in the EduProtocols community on Facebook.

Jon is only an educator because of his amazing wife. She started the whole project that changed his life. After not once encouraging his kids to be in education, Nolan, Mia, and Claire are all in education-based jobs. Life is funny that way.

Jon lives near Yosemite and spends his free time as the head maintenance person for the family Airbnbs. Yes, there's a teacher discount. Just email him to access it.

The EduProtocol Field Guide Math Edition by Lisa Nowakowski and Jeremiah Ruesch
The EduProtocol Field Guide Primary Edition by Benjamin Cogswell and Jennifer Dean
The EduProtocol Field Guide Social Studies Edition by Dr. Scott M. Petri and Adam Moler

Leadership & School Culture

Autopilot by Rich Czyz
Be 1% Better by Ron Clark
Be THAT Teacher by Dwayne Reed
Beyond the Surface of Restorative Practices by Marisol Rerucha
Change the Narrative by Henry J. Turner and Kathy Lopes
Choosing to See by Pamela Seda and Kyndall Brown
Culturize by Jimmy Casas
Discipline Win by Andy Jacks
Educate Me! by Dr. Shree Walker with Michael D. Ison
Escaping the School Leader's Dunk Tank by Rebecca Coda and Rick Jetter
Fight Song by Kim Bearden
From Teacher to Leader by Starr Sackstein
If the Dance Floor Is Empty, Change the Song by Joe Clark
The Innovator's Mindset by George Couros
It's OK to Say "They" by Christy Whittlesey
Kids Deserve It! by Todd Nesloney and Adam Welcome
Leading the Whole Teacher by Allyson Apsey
Let Them Speak by Rebecca Coda and Rick Jetter
The Limitless School by Abe Hege and Adam Dovico
Live Your Excellence by Jimmy Casas
Next-Level Teaching by Jonathan Alsheimer
The Pepper Effect by Sean Gaillard
Principaled by Kate Barker, Kourtney Ferrua, and Rachael George
The Principled Principal by Jeffrey Zoul and Anthony McConnell
Relentless by Hamish Brewer
The Secret Solution by Todd Whitaker, Sam Miller, and Ryan Donlan
Start. Right. Now. by Todd Whitaker, Jeffrey Zoul, and Jimmy Casas
Stop. Right. Now. by Jimmy Casas and Jeffrey Zoul
Teach Your Class Off by CJ Reynolds
Teachers Deserve It by Rae Hughart and Adam Welcome
They Call Me "Mr. De" by Frank DeAngelis
Thrive through the Five by Jill M. Siler

Unmapped Potential by Julie Hasson and Missy Lennard

When Kids Lead by Todd Nesloney and Adam Dovico

Word Shift by Joy Kirr

Your School Rocks by Ryan McLane and Eric Lowe

Technology & Tools

50 Things to Go Further with Google Classroom by Alice Keeler and Libbi Miller

50 Things You Can Do with Google Classroom by Alice Keeler and Libbi Miller

50 Ways to Engage Students with Google Apps by Alice Keeler and Heather Lyon

140 Twitter Tips for Educators by Brad Currie, Billy Krakower, and Scott Rocco

AI Optimism by Becky Keene

Block Breaker by Brian Aspinall

Building Blocks for Tiny Techies by Jamila "Mia" Leonard

Code Breaker by Brian Aspinall

The Complete EdTech Coach by Katherine Goyette and Adam Juarez

Control Alt Achieve by Eric Curts

The Esports Education Playbook by Chris Aviles, Steve Isaacs, Christine Lion-Bailey, and Jesse Lubinsky

Google Apps for Littles by Christine Pinto and Alice Keeler

Master the Media by Julie Smith

Raising Digital Leaders by Jennifer Casa-Todd

Reality Bytes by Christine Lion-Bailey, Jesse Lubinsky, and Micah Shippee, PhD

Sail the 7 Cs with Microsoft Education by Becky Keene and Kathi Kersznowski

Shake Up Learning by Kasey Bell

Social LEADia by Jennifer Casa-Todd

Stepping Up to Google Classroom by Alice Keeler and Kimberly Mattina

Teaching Math with Google Apps by Alice Keeler and Diana Herrington

Teaching with Google Jamboard by Alice Keeler and Kimberly Mattina

Teachingland by Amanda Fox and Mary Ellen Weeks

Teaching Methods & Materials

All 4s and 5s by Andrew Sharos

Boredom Busters by Katie Powell

Building Strong Writers by Christina Schneider

The Classroom Chef by John Stevens and Matt Vaudrey

The Collaborative Classroom by Trevor Muir

Copyrighteous by Diana Gill

CREATE by Bethany J. Petty
Ditch That Homework by Matt Miller and Alice Keeler
Ditch That Textbook by Matt Miller
Don't Ditch That Tech by Matt Miller, Nate Ridgway, and Angelia Ridgway
EDrenaline Rush by John Meehan
Educated by Design by Michael Cohen, The Tech Rabbi
Empowered to Choose: A Practical Guide to Personalized Learning by Andrew Easton
Expedition Science by Becky Schnekser
Frustration Busters by Katie Powell
Fully Engaged by Michael Matera and John Meehan
Game On? Brain On! by Lindsay Portnoy, PhD
Guided Math AMPED by Reagan Tunstall
Happy & Resilient by Roni Habib
Innovating Play by Jessica LaBar-Twomy and Christine Pinto
Instant Relevance by Denis Sheeran
Instructional Coaching Connection by Nathan Lang-Raad
Keeping the Wonder by Jenna Copper, Ashley Bible, Abby Gross, and Staci Lamb
LAUNCH by John Spencer and A.J. Juliani
Learning in the Zone by Dr. Sonny Magana
Less Talk, More Action by Allyson Apsey and Emily Freeland
Lights, Cameras, TEACH! by Kevin J. Butler
Make Learning MAGICAL by Tisha Richmond
The Magical CTE Classroom by Tisha Richmond
Pass the Baton by Kathryn Finch and Theresa Hoover
Playing with Purpose by MIchael Matera & John Meehan
Project-Based Learning Anywhere by Lori Elliott
Pure Genius by Don Wettrick
The Revolution by Darren Ellwein and Derek McCoy
The Science Box by Kim Adsit and Adam Peterson
Shift This! by Joy Kirr
Skyrocket Your Teacher Coaching by Michael Cary Sonbert
Spark Learning by Ramsey Musallam
Sparks in the Dark by Travis Crowder and Todd Nesloney
Table Talk Math by John Stevens
Teachables by Cheryl Abla and Lisa Maxfield
Unpack Your Impact by Naomi O'Brien and LaNesha Tabb
The Wild Card by Hope and Wade King

Writefully Empowered by Jacob Chastain
The Writing on the Classroom Wall by Steve Wyborney
You Are Poetry by Mike Johnston
You'll Never Guess What I'm Saying by Naomi O'Brien
You'll Never Guess What I'm Thinking About by Naomi O'Brien

Inspiration, Professional Growth & Personal Development

Becoming the BISON by Kim Gameroz
Be REAL by Tara Martin
Be the One for Kids by Ryan Sheehy
The Coach ADVenture by Amy Illingworth
Creatively Productive by Lisa Johnson
The Ed Branding Book by Dr. Renae Bryant and Lynette White
Educational Eye Exam by Alicia Ray
The EduNinja Mindset by Jennifer Burdis
Empower Our Girls by Lynmara Colón and Adam Welcome
Finding Lifelines by Andrew Grieve and Andrew Sharos
The Four O'Clock Faculty by Rich Czyz
How Much Water Do We Have? by Pete and Kris Nunweiler
P Is for Pirate by Dave and Shelley Burgess
A Passion for Kindness by Tamara Letter
The Path to Serendipity by Allyson Apsey
PheMOMenal Teacher by Annick Rauch
Recipes for Resilience by Robert A. Martinez
Rogue Leader by Rich Czyz
Sanctuaries by Dan Tricarico
Saving Sycamore by Molly B. Hudgens
The Secret Sauce by Rich Czyz
Shattering the Perfect Teacher Myth by Aaron Hogan
Stories from Webb by Todd Nesloney
Talk to Me by Kim Bearden
Teach Better by Chad Ostrowski, Tiffany Ott, Rae Hughart, and Jeff Gargas
Teacher by Day by Dr. Yvette Dixon Ledford
Teach Me, Teacher by Jacob Chastain
Teach, Play, Learn! by Adam Peterson
The Teachers of Oz by Herbie Raad and Nathan Lang-Raad
Teaching Is a Tattoo by Mike Johnston

Teaching the Ms. Abbott Way by Joyce Stephens Abbott
TeamMakers by Laura Robb and Evan Robb
Through the Lens of Serendipity by Allyson Apsey
Write Here and Now by Dan Tricarico
The Zen Teacher by Dan Tricarico

Children's Books

Alpert by LaNesha Tabb
Alpert Becomes an Author by LaNesha Tabb
Alpert Finds a Problem by LaNesha Tabb
Alpert & Friends by LaNesha Tabb
Beyond Us by Aaron Polansky
Cannonball In by Tara Martin
Dolphins in Trees by Aaron Polansky
Dragon Smart by Tisha and Tommy Richmond
I Can Achieve Anything by MoNique Waters
I Want to Be a Lot by Ashley Savage
The Magic of Wonder by Jenna Copper, Ashley Bible, Abby Gross, and Staci Lamb
Micah's Big Question by Naomi O'Brien
The Princes of Serendip by Allyson Apsey
Ride with Emilio by Richard Nares
A Teacher's Top Secret Confidential by LaNesha Tabb
A Teacher's Top Secret: Mission Accomplished by LaNesha Tabb
The Wild Card Kids by Hope and Wade King
Zom-Be a Design Thinker by Amanda Fox

www.ingramcontent.com/pod-product-compliance
Lightning Source LLC
La Vergne TN
LVHW081323110826
845149LV00007B/1576
9781968898199